Simple Sewing

Simple Sewing

30 Fast and Easy Projects for Beginners

Katie Lewis

PLAIN SIGHT PUBLISHING,
AN IMPRINT OF CEDAR FORT, INC.
SPRINGVILLE, UTAH

© 2013 Katie Lewis
Step-by-step photography by Katie Lewis
Cover and project photography by Suzanne Gipson

ISBN 13: 978-1-4621-1288-3

Published by Plain Sight Publishing, an imprint of Cedar Fort, Inc.
2373 W. 700 S., Springville, UT 84663
Distributed by Cedar Fort, Inc., www.cedarfort.com

Library of Congress Cataloging-in-Publication Data on file

Cover and page design by Angela D. Olsen
Cover design © 2013 by Lyle Mortimer
Edited by Whitney A. Lindsley and Eileen Leavitt

Printed in the United States of America

10 9 8 7 6 5 4 3 2 1

Dedication

To my mother, who taught me how to sew. And write.

To my husband, Bryan, who has supported me every step along the way. You have always treated my hobbies with as much respect as your own career, and for that I love you deeply.

And to my daughter, Olivia. Let's make more bean bags together.

Acknowledgments

Special thanks to the friendly and helpful staff at Sew to Speak in Columbus, Ohio, for their gorgeous selection of fabric and sewing materials and for their continuous help and support.

Thanks also to Suzanne Gipson, who took all of the beautiful staged project photos and cover photos for the book.

Thanks to my friend Abby Smith for allowing us to photograph the ballerina doll I made from her "Ruby Lou Doll" pattern.

Heartfelt thanks to my mother, my husband, my good friend Laura Hatch, and several other friends and family members who tested and read early drafts of the projects in this book. Their help and feedback has been invaluable.

And my deep love and gratitude to my brother David who opened his mouth and told someone, "Hey, my sister's writing a sewing book." This book is published and sitting on the shelf because of his continued selflessness and love.

Contents

A Note from the Author

I first learned how to sew as a child on my mother's old brown Singer sewing machine. I sat on a funky old square stool and turned the hand wheel, stitch by stitch, because I was too afraid to use the foot pedal. My specialty at the time was bean bags. I loved sewing the fabric together, filling them up with beans, and then playing with the new bean bag. I was always amazed by the idea that I could make something all by myself that was actually sturdy and useful. It filled me with a great sense of wonder and accomplishment.

Now, years later, I still feel that sense of deep wonder and accomplishment every time I finish a new project. I've taught several sewing classes over the years and my favorite part is when a friend who is new to sewing beams down at their newly finished projects and says, "I made this!" I hope you will feel that excitement as you build your sewing skills and create the projects from this book. Additionally, I hope that once you've mastered the basic skills taught here, you'll feel empowered to change and embellish these projects to fit your own needs and personality.

I have specifically designed the projects in this book to be genuinely easy for beginners to complete, to hold up well over time, and to be truly useful. Be sure to read through the opening section, *Before You Begin*, for a brief description of the tools, materials, and techniques used for the projects in this book. This section will help you know how to use your tools correctly and what materials to look for at the store. The photographed step-by-step instructions will guide you through each project. Still, if there's ever a step you're having trouble with, don't hesitate to ask a friend. A good sewing friend is one of the most valuable tools to keep in your sewing toolbox.

Now it's time to jump right in! Gather your supplies and get to work!

Happy sewing!

Katie Lewis

Before You Begin

- Sewing Supplies

- Fabric

- Stitches

- Terms & Techniques

SEWING SUPPLIES

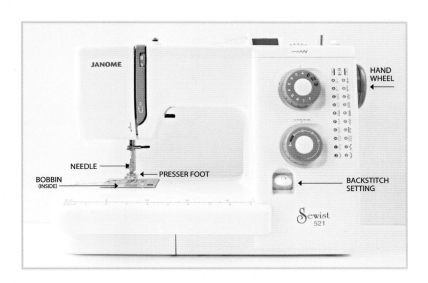

Sewing machine

Every sewing machine is different, but you should know a few basic things about your machine before you start sewing. Refer to your user manual to familiarize yourself with the layout of your machine. Be sure you can locate and operate the needle, bobbin, presser foot, hand wheel, backstitch setting, and foot pedal. Also read in your manual to learn how to correctly thread your sewing machine and how to wind and insert a new bobbin.

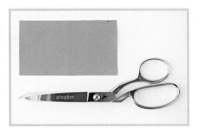

Sewing scissors

Basic sewing scissors, sometimes referred to as sewing shears, are sharper than typical scissors. Use your sewing scissors to cut fabric or to trim threads. Do not use them on paper. If you do, the blades will dull over time.

Pinking shears

Pinking shears have blades that are zigzagged. Use your pinking shears to trim seam allowances on curved items to reduce bulk. Pinking shears can also be used to finish seam allowances to keep them from fraying too much or to create a decorative trim. As with your regular sewing scissors, do not use them on paper.

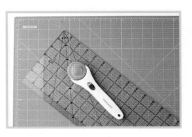

Rotary cutter, ruler, and mat

The best way to get a straight cut on a flat piece of fabric is to cut with a rotary cutter and acrylic ruler on top of a cutting mat.

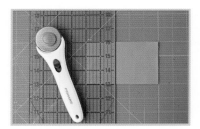

To use your rotary cutter, align your fabric with the lines on the cutting mat and place the acrylic ruler on top, making sure the ruler is carefully aligned with the appropriate measurements on each end of the mat.

Press down firmly on the ruler with your left hand and hold the rotary cutter in your right hand. Unlock the safety on your rotary cutter. While pressing down firmly on the ruler, press the edge of the rotary cutter blade up against the edge of the ruler. With the blade touching the edge of the ruler, press the rotary cutter down firmly into the fabric as you roll the blade away from you to make your cut. Once you've made your cut, continue to hold the ruler in place while you pull the excess fabric away. If any part of the fabric is still connected, make the cut again. Always cut away from yourself when using a rotary cutter. Do not roll the blade back and forth across the fabric. This will not make a straight cut and could cause an injury.

Iron & ironing board

One of the best things you can do to make your handmade items look more professional is to iron and press them. Before you begin a project, iron the fabric by moving your iron back and forth across the fabric to eliminate any creases. Throughout each project, press your seams and folds by holding the iron in place along the area you wish to press. Pressing can be used to help keep edges looking crisp and to create a temporary line in the fabric to guide you as you sew.

When appropriate for the fabric you are using, lightly spraying your fabric with water before you iron or using the steam setting on your iron can help eliminate unwanted creases and will make your fabric extra crisp and nice as you press. If you are unsure whether to use water on your fabric, test it on a corner or scrap first.

Different kinds of fabric need to be ironed and pressed at different temperatures. Be sure the setting on your iron is appropriate for the fabric you are using. Appropriate settings for the fabric used for the projects in this book are noted in the section on fabric on pages 5–6.

Pins

Pins are used to hold two pieces of fabric together in preparation for sewing. Regular straight pins are best for the projects in this book.

Thread

There are many different kinds of thread, all in a wide variety of colors. Use all-purpose thread when sewing the projects in this book. If you want the stitching to show on your project, choose a contrasting color of thread. If you want the stitching to blend in with your project, match the color of thread to the color of fabric you'll be using for your project. Coats & Clark makes a great line of high quality all-purpose thread that comes in a variety of colors and is very affordable.

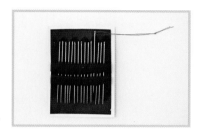

Hand sewing needle

Use a basic, sharp hand-sewing needle when completing any hand-sewing for the projects in this book. Embroidery and cross-stitch needles are too big.

Seam ripper

A seam ripper is used to unpick your sewing mistakes. To use, slip the point of the seam ripper under an unwanted stitch and then push the base of the U-shaped part of the seam ripper up against the thread. The thread will break, allowing you to pull out the stitch. Continue breaking the thread one or two stitches at a time until the unwanted seam is removed. Always be sure that you are only ripping through the thread and not through the fabric.

If you only need to remove part of a seam, unpick only the unwanted area. Then, starting at the stitching that is still intact, backstitch over the existing stitching, sew a new seam across the open area, and sew over the next line of stitching, making sure to backstitch again.

Chopstick/crochet hook

Use the tip of a chopstick or small crochet hook to help push corners into place when you turn your projects right side out. It's okay to push firmly, but be careful not to push too hard or you could break through the stitching.

Buttons

There are so many wonderful varieties of buttons to choose from. The only project in this book that requires a button is the Pillow Pincushion on page 59, which uses a ½˝ button, meaning the button is ½˝ in diameter.

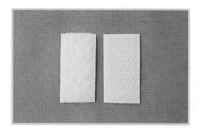

Velcro

Velcro is a hook and loop fastener made up of two separate pieces—a soft side and a scratchy side. When the two sides of the Velcro touch, they stick together. To open the Velcro, simply pull the two sides apart. The Velcro used for the projects in this book is ¾˝ wide.

Stuffing

There are several different kinds of basic stuffing available. Any kind will work well for the projects in this book.

FABRIC

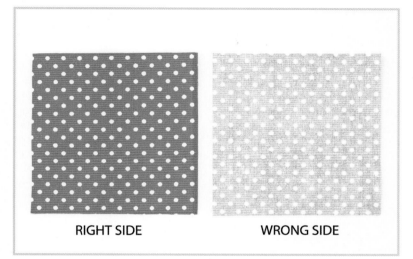

RIGHT SIDE   WRONG SIDE

Right side versus wrong side

Most kinds of fabric have a right side and a wrong side. If the fabric has a print, the side where the print shows clearly is the right side, and the side where the print is muted or harder to see is the wrong side. Plain-colored quilting cotton doesn't really have a right side or a wrong side since it looks the same on both sides. This is also true for fabric where the design is woven in, rather than printed on. The right side of each kind of fabric used in this book is noted in the following descriptions.

Quilting cotton

Quilting cotton is a woven fabric. It is usually 100 percent cotton, and it comes in a wide variety of solid colors and prints. Always wash new quilting cotton before sewing with it. This will prevent your project from shrinking in the wash later on. For quilting cotton with a print, the printed side is the right side of the fabric. For quilting cotton that is made of 100 percent cotton, use the cotton setting on your iron.

Flannel

Flannel is a woven fabric that is soft on one side. Like quilting cotton, flannel also comes in a wide variety of solid colors and prints and is usually 100 percent cotton. Always wash new flannel before sewing with it. This will prevent your project from shrinking in the wash later on. The right side of flannel is the soft side. For flannel that is 100 percent cotton, use the cotton setting on your iron.

Felt

Felt is a synthetic fabric made by fusing fibers together. It's a fun material to use because it has no right or wrong side, and the edges won't fray when you cut it. Craft felt is acrylic and will pill much more over time than wool felt. When a fabric pills, it creates little balls of material on the surface of the fabric. Wool felt is made of wool or a wool blend and is sturdier than craft felt. Both craft felt and wool felt can be bought in small sheets or by the yard. In general, it's best not to wash, iron, or press felt. If you do need to iron or press it, use the lowest setting on your iron and test on a scrap first.

Terrycloth

Terrycloth is the kind of fabric that towels are made from. Always wash new terry cloth before sewing with it. This will prevent your project from shrinking in the wash later on. For some terrycloth, the right side of terrycloth has lots of tiny little loops, called pile, and the wrong side is flat. For other kinds of terrycloth, the pile shows on both sides, so that there is no right or wrong side. Raw edges of terrycloth will fray quite a bit, so take care as you cut and handle it. Ironing terrycloth can flatten the pile, making it less fluffy. Iron and press terrycloth when necessary using the cotton setting on your iron.

Chalk cloth

Chalk cloth is just what it sounds like—fabric that you can write on like a chalkboard. The right side of chalk cloth is the chalkboard side and the wrong side is bumpy and has fused threads showing. The wrong side of chalk cloth cannot be written on. Unlike any of the other fabric used for the projects in this book, chalk cloth will pin mark easily. This means that once you poke a pin or needle through it, the hole made by the pin or needle will always be visible, so take extra care when pinning. Do not wash, iron, or press chalk cloth. If you need to flatten a rolled or creased piece of chalk cloth, lay it flat under some heavy books overnight.

Once your chalk cloth is sewn onto your project, you will need to prime it by rubbing the side of a piece of chalk over the entire chalk cloth. Erase the chalk coating and your chalk cloth is ready to write on. Only use chalk to write on chalk cloth. Look for chalk cloth in the utility fabric section at your local fabric store.

⬤ STITCHES

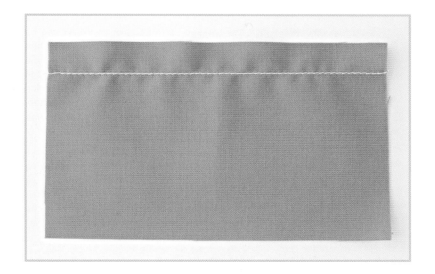

Straight stitch

A straight stitch is the basic stitch you will use when sewing all of the projects in this book. For the projects in this book, make sure your straight stitch is set to a standard length, about 2–2 ½ mm.

Back stitching

Backstitching is sewing a straight stitch forward and backward for 2 to 3 stitches. Do this when you begin or end a new seam so the stitching won't unravel.

Edgestitching

Edgestitching is sewing a straight stitch ⅛˝ away from the edge of the fabric. Always edgestitch with the front of the project facing up.

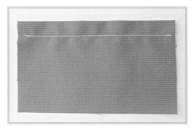

Topstitching

Topstitching is a general term for a decorative stitch sewn on top of a finished project. Though it does not create a seam, it can add strength to existing seams, making it especially appropriate for use around the top edge of bags. Always topstitch with the front of the project facing up. The topstitching used for the projects in this book is always a straight stitch sewn ½˝ away from the edge.

TERMS & TECHNIQUES

Pinning flat items

Believe it or not, there is a right way to pin fabric together, and pinning correctly will help keep your fabric more accurately aligned, leading to a nicer finished product. Pinning correctly can feel awkward at first, but keep at it and soon it will come naturally.

When pinning flat items, bring them to a hard, flat surface, such as a cutting mat. Pinning on top of a rotary cutting mat works especially well because you won't be in danger of scratching the surface with your pins like you would if you were working on a kitchen table. When pinning on a cutting mat, it can also be helpful to align the straight edges of the fabric pieces you are pinning with the lines on the cutting mat. This way you will be sure the edges of your fabric are straight as you pin.

Once your fabric is on a hard, flat surface and the edges of the fabric pieces are aligned, you're ready to pin. Without picking up the fabric, hold the fabric in place and insert a pin down through both layers of fabric. You'll know when the pin has gone through both layers because the tip of the pin will hit the hard surface.

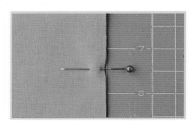

Then, keeping the fabric flat, poke the pin back up through both layers of fabric. At no time during the pinning process should your hands be underneath the fabric being pinned.

Not all projects in this book can be pinned this way. For example, when pinning around the top of a bag, you will need to hold the fabric pieces in your hands as you pin. When pinning on top of a flat surface isn't an option, just do your best to keep edges and seams aligned.

As you sew your projects, remove your pins one at a time before sewing over them. It's generally a good rule of thumb to remove each pin when it gets to be about 1–2˝ away from the needle on the sewing machine. Never sew over your pins. Doing so can cause both your pins and the needle on your sewing machine to break.

Pinning stuffed items

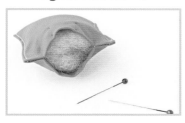

For several of the projects in this book you will be instructed to pin the edge of an item that is stuffed with stuffing, rice, or beans. In all cases, move the stuffing, rice, or beans away from the edge being pinned.

Pull the open edge taut between your fingers.

Keeping the open edge taut between your fingers, insert the pin into the open edge the same way you would if it were a flat item.

Then, instead of letting the sharp point of the pin rest on top of the fabric like you normally would, insert the point directly back in through the top layer of fabric so the point of the pin is sticking straight into the stuffing, between the two layers of fabric.

Inserting the pins this way will help keep the pinned edge flat while you sew. It will also help keep the stuffing away from the pinned edge as you sew.

Seam allowance

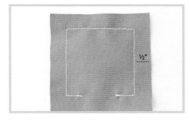

The seam allowance is the distance between the edge of the fabric and the stitching line. All of the seam allowances for the projects in this book are ½″.

Starting to stitch

One of the most common and most frustrating sewing mistakes is when you start to sew a new row of stitching and your thread ends get all bunched up under your fabric in a big, jumbled mess. In some cases, this can even cause your sewing machine to jam. To avoid this mistake, follow these two simple rules whenever you begin sewing a new seam:

First, rather than starting to sew right at the edge of your fabric, always begin sewing about ½″ in from the edge of the fabric. You can backstitch to cover the ½″ that you skipped, but starting a little further in will keep the edge of your fabric from getting sucked down into the machine.

Second, always hold on to your thread ends as you start. Before you start to sew, position the fabric, put the presser foot down, and use your right hand to hold on firmly to the thread ends. While holding on tight to the thread ends, start sewing the first few stitches. Once you sew these first few stitches, you can let go of the thread ends as you backstitch, and then continue to sew your project.

Clipping thread ends

When you sew a row of stitching, you will always have a bit of extra thread at the beginning of the row of stitching and at the end. Taking the extra threads one at a time, pull them straight, and snip the extra thread right at the surface of the fabric, next to the stitching.

Not only will this keep your thread ends from getting tangled together as you sew, but it will also improve the overall look of your finished project.

Clipping the corners

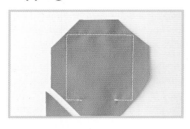

Most of the projects in this book begin by instructing you to sew around the edge of the fabric and then to clip the corners. Clipping corners is done to reduce bulk so that when you turn your project right side out, you will be able to push the corners nicely into place.

To clip the corners, make a straight cut diagonally across each of the corners. Cut very close to the stitching lines (about ⅛" away), but do not cut through the stitching.

Pull seam edges out before pressing

Ideally, it's always best to press a seam open so the fabric doesn't pucker, but this isn't always possible for the projects in this book. Instead, here's a little trick to keep your seams neat and tidy:

After you turn your project right side out, the seams will fold slightly in on themselves instead of lying straight and neat like you want them to.

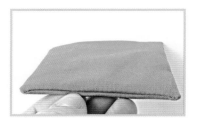

To fix this, use your fingernails to roll the seams out into place.

Once you've pulled the seam into place, press the edge to keep everything nice and straight.

How to copy patterns

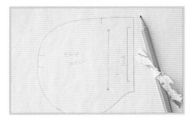

Some of the projects in this book require the use of patterns. Do not cut these patterns out of the book. Instead, trace the patterns using a pencil and tracing paper or tissue paper. All of the patterns included in this book are sized at 100 percent, so you do not need to resize them before tracing.

To trace a pattern, place a piece of tracing paper or tissue paper directly on top of the pattern you want to trace. Then use a pencil to carefully trace the outline of the pattern. Be sure to copy any markings included on the pattern.

Some of the larger patterns are split up onto multiple pages. Copy each piece of the pattern, and then tape the pieces together using the markings on the pattern as your guide.

Use your new traced pattern to cut and prepare the fabric pieces for your project.

Mark a seam allowance on your sewing machine

Most sewing machines have several measurements marked right on the sewing machine so you can keep your fabric straight as you sew. However, if your sewing machine doesn't have a certain marking or if you just want to mark a seam allowance so it shows up more easily, adding a piece of tape is a great temporary fix. Masking tape or washi tape both work well.

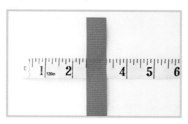

To mark a ½˝ seam allowance on your sewing machine, start by cutting a piece of tape about 3˝ long. With the tape running perpendicular to the ruler, place the edge of the tape on top of the 2 ½˝ mark on the ruler.

Move the needle on your sewing machine so it's in the down position. Position the ruler so the 2˝ mark is aligned with the needle on your sewing machine. Carefully press the top end of the tape onto your sewing machine so it sticks.

Holding the tape end in place on the sewing machine, carefully remove the ruler, and continue pressing the rest of the tape onto the sewing machine. Double check your work with the ruler to make sure that the edge of your tape is ½˝ away from the sewing machine needle.

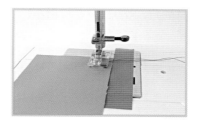

Now, with your tape in place, whenever you want to sew something with a ½˝ seam allowance, you can simply line up the edge of the fabric with the edge of the tape.

You can also use this method for marking an ⅛˝ seam allowance directly onto the presser foot to use as a guide for edgestitching. Instead of using a 3˝ piece of tape, use a small, skinny piece of tape, no longer than 1˝. Once the edge of the tape is in place ⅛˝ from the sewing machine needle, trim away any excess tape hanging off the edge of the presser foot so it doesn't stick to the fabric as you sew. With the ⅛˝ seam allowance marked directly on the presser foot, you can edgestitch easily and accurately without having to measure as you go.

How to sew on a button

Just like there's a right way to pin fabric together, there's also a right way to sew on a button. The good news is that it's easy to do, will make your button stay nice and sturdy, and looks great once you've finished.

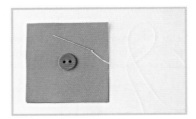

Start by threading a hand-sewing needle. Fold the thread in half, with the needle resting at the fold. Tie the thread ends together into a knot.

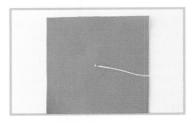

With the top of the fabric facing up, poke the needle down through the fabric. You should be poking the needle down through the center of where you want your button to be. Continue pulling the needle and thread through the fabric until the knot is flush with the top of the fabric.

From the backside of the fabric, poke the needle back up through the fabric about ⅛″ away from the previous stitch.

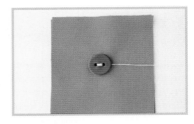

Thread the button onto the needle and move it down the thread until the button is in place on top of the fabric. Sew down through the opposite buttonhole, then back up through the first button hole. Continue sewing through these first two holes 3–4 times. If your button has four holes, sew through the remaining two holes 3–4 times. After sewing down through the button for the last time, poke the needle back up through the top layer of fabric underneath the button, and pull the thread tight.

Pull the button up slightly and make a small stitch underneath the button where the stitch won't be seen.

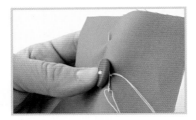

Tie a small knot next to the stitch under the button, flush with the top of the fabric. Then, right next to the knot you just tied, poke the needle in between both layers of fabric and bring the needle out through the top fabric about 1″ away from the button.

Pull the thread tight and cut the thread right at the surface of the fabric. The thread ends will hide neatly inside, and your button will securely stay in place.

Projects

Chapter One

Accessories

SIMPLE BOW

This simple bow is fast and easy to whip up. Wear it in your hair or use it as a bow tie. The instructions are the same for both!

You will need:

- ⅛ yard quilting cotton for the FRONT, BACK, and LOOP

- 1 double prong alligator clip

- All-purpose thread

Tip: If you don't want to buy the full ⅛ yard of fabric, buy 1 fat quarter instead. Fat quarters of fabric typically measure about 18″ × 22″ and often come precut. If you can't find precut fat quarters at your fabric shop you can always ask if they'll cut one for you at the cutting counter.

Yield: 1 bow

Prepare the following pieces:

FRONT—4″ tall x 12″ wide

BACK—4″ tall x 12″ wide

LOOP—3½″ tall x 2½″ wide

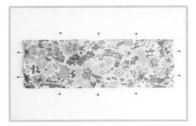

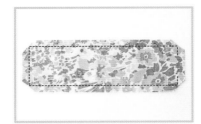

Step 1: Pin FRONT to BACK

With the FRONT and BACK right sides together, measure 1˝ from each corner along the right edge and pin. The space between these two pins will mark where the opening will be when you sew. Continue pinning around the bow.

Step 2: Sew FRONT to BACK

Starting at one end of the opening, backstitch and sew around the bow using a ½˝ seam allowance. Stop and backstitch at the other end of the opening.

Step 3: Clip corners

Snip off the corners of the bow, making sure not to cut through the stitching.

Step 4: Turn bow right side out and press

Turn the bow right side out.

Use a chopstick to gently push the corners into place. Press the bow to keep the edges crisp.

Step 5: Mark center

Fold the bow in half and press the fold.

Step 6: Open fold

Open the fold with the back of the bow facing up.

Step 7: Fold right edge in

With the back of the bow facing up, fold the right edge of the bow in to the center fold and pin in place.

Step 8: Edgestitch along pinned edge

Edgestitch along the pinned edge, making sure to backstitch as you start and stop.

Step 9: Pin and sew remaining edge

Repeat steps 7 and 8 for the left edge of the bow.

Step 10: Prepare LOOP edges

With the wrong side of the LOOP facing up, fold each long (3½˝) edge over ½˝ and press.

Step 11: Fold LOOP in half

Fold the LOOP in half lengthwise. Make sure the folded edges are aligned, and pin them in place.

Step 12: Edgestitch along sides of LOOP

Edgestitch along each of the long (3½˝) edges of the LOOP, making sure to backstitch as you start and stop.

Step 13: Fold LOOP ends

Fold each of the short, raw ends of the LOOP under ½˝ and press.

Step 14: Position LOOP on back of bow

With the LOOP facing up, position the top end of the LOOP at the center of the back of the bow and pin in place.

Step 15: Sew LOOP in place

Edgestitch along the top edge of the LOOP, making sure to backstitch as you start and stop.

Step 16: Prepare to wrap LOOP around bow

Lift the LOOP up to reveal the raw end.

Step 17: Fold into bow shape

Fold the bottom edge of the bow up to the middle of the bow, covering the raw edge of the LOOP.

Fold the top edge of the bow down to the middle of the bow.

Step 18: Wrap LOOP around bow

Wrap the LOOP down under the bottom of the bow. Continue to wrap the LOOP around the middle of the bow until the remaining folded end covers the stitching line from step 15.

Pin the remaining folded end of the LOOP in place by sticking a pin straight through the middle of the bow.

Step 19: Slipstitch part 1

Thread a hand-sewing needle with about half an arm's length of thread.

Tie the thread ends together into a knot to create a double layer of thread.

Move the needle to the center of the thread with the knot at the opposite end.

Insert the needle up through the bottom of the LOOP about ⅛″ away from the right edge.

Pull the needle until the thread is tight.

Step 20: Slipstitch part 2

Make a small stitch (about ⅛″ long) through the folded edge of the LOOP and pull the thread tight. Note that you should not be pulling the thread so tight that the fabric bunches up, but just tight enough to keep the thread straight.

Step 21: Slipstitch part 3

Make another small stitch through the bottom layer of the LOOP just below the place where the previous stitch ended and pull the thread tight.

Step 22: Slipstitch part 4

Continue to alternate making a stitch through the top edge of the LOOP and the bottom layer of the LOOP until it is sewn all the way across. Be sure to pull the thread tight with each stitch.

Step 23: Tie knot

Make a small stitch through the left edge of the LOOP. Before pulling the thread tight, insert the needle through the loop created by the stitch. This will create a small knot. Pull the thread tight.

Repeat this step to create another small knot.

Do not cut the thread.

Step 24: Hide thread ends

Insert the needle into the left edge of the LOOP and poke it out through the center of the LOOP.

Step 25: Cut thread ends

Pull the thread tight and cut the thread flush against the fabric. The thread ends will hide neatly inside the LOOP.

Step 26: Add alligator clip

Open the alligator clip and slip the top portion through the LOOP at the back of the bow.

If desired, add a small amount of hot glue to the alligator clip before slipping it into place.

Finished!

To use as a bow tie:

Open the alligator clip and slip the bottom prongs behind the top button of the shirt.

Tuck the points of the collar under the bow.

BASIC TOTE BAG

A great, basic tote bag is sure to be used over and over again—and for a million different things! This sturdy tote bag is large enough to hold library books or groceries, and stylish enough to toss your wallet into and use as a purse!

You will need:

- ½ yard quilting cotton for the OUTER and the STRAPS

- ½ yard quilting cotton for the LINING

- All-purpose thread

Yield: 1 tote bag

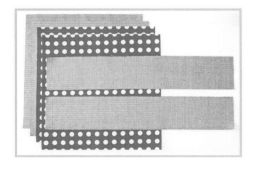

Prepare the following pieces:

OUTER FRONT and BACK—14˝ tall × 14˝ wide

LINING FRONT and BACK—14˝ tall × 14˝ wide

STRAPS—4˝ tall × 22˝ wide (cut 2 straps)

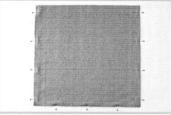

Step 1: Pin OUTER FRONT to OUTER BACK

Pin the OUTER FRONT to the OUTER BACK with the right sides together along the bottom and side edges. Do not pin across the top edge.

Step 2: Sew FRONT to BACK

Sew along one side, across the bottom, and along the remaining side using a ½″ seam allowance. Make sure to backstitch as you start and stop.

Step 3: Clip corners

Snip off the bottom corners of the OUTER, making sure not to cut through the stitching.

Step 4: Fold and press top edge

Fold the top edge over ½″ all the way around and press.

Step 5: Create LINING

Repeat steps 1–4 to create the LINING.

Step 6: Turn OUTER right side out and press

Turn the OUTER right side out.

Use a chopstick to gently push the corners into place. Press the OUTER to keep the edges crisp. Keep the fold along the opening tucked neatly inside as you press.

Do not turn the LINING right side out.

7

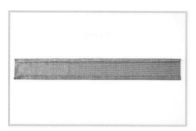

Step 7: Prepare STRAP edges

Place a STRAP on the ironing board with the wrong side facing up.

Fold each long (22″) edge over ½″ and press.

8

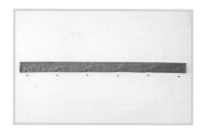

Step 8: Fold STRAP

Fold the entire STRAP in half lengthwise, making sure the folded edges from step 7 are aligned.

Press all the way along the new fold.

Pin the STRAP along the open edge.

9

Step 9: Sew STRAP

Edgestitch along both long (22″) edges of the STRAP, making sure to backstitch as you start and stop.

10

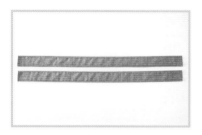

Step 10: Create remaining STRAP

Repeat steps 7–9 to create the remaining STRAP.

11

Step 11: Pin STRAP to OUTER FRONT

Unfold the top edge of the OUTER.

With the top of the STRAP facing down, position the outside edge of the strap 3″ from the side seam and pin in place on the OUTER FRONT. Measure in 3″ from the opposite side seam and pin the remaining end of the STRAP in place.

As you pin, be sure to only pin through the top layer of the OUTER FRONT. Do not pin through both layers of the OUTER.

12

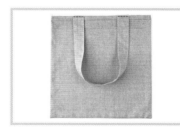

Step 12: Sew STRAP to OUTER FRONT

Edgestitch along both ends of the STRAP, making sure to backstitch as you start and stop.

As you sew, be sure to only sew through the OUTER FRONT. Do not sew through both layers of the OUTER.

Repeat steps 11–12 to attach the remaining STRAP to the OUTER BACK.

Step 13: Refold and press top edge

With both straps sewn to the top edge of the OUTER, refold the top edge of the OUTER along the original ½″ fold line. The straps should now be sticking straight up out of the OUTER.

Press along the fold again to keep the top edge crisp.

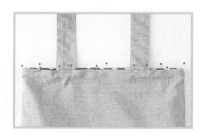

Step 14: Pin LINING inside OUTER

Insert the LINING inside the OUTER. Match the side seams and the folded edge along the top of the OUTER and LINING, and pin the LINING in place all the way around the bag opening.

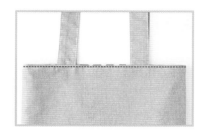

Step 15: Edgestitch around opening

Start at a side seam and edgestitch around the entire opening of the bag, making sure to backstitch as you start and stop. The purpose of this edgestitching is to attach the LINING to the OUTER. Do not sew the opening shut.

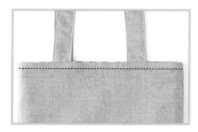

Step 16: Topstitch around opening

Start at a side seam and topstitch around the entire opening of the bag ½″ from the top edge, making sure to backstitch as you start and stop. This extra row of stitching will add to the strength of your bag.

Finished!

SUNGLASSES CASE

Stop your sunglasses from getting lost and scratched in the bottom of your purse by keeping them in this soft case. Just slip them in for easy storage, and pop them out when you're ready for some sun!

You will need:

- ¼ yard quilting cotton for the OUTER
- ¼ yard quilting cotton for the LINING
- All-purpose thread

Tip: If you don't want to buy the full ¼ yard of fabric for the OUTER or LINING, buy 1 fat quarter for each instead. Fat quarters of fabric typically measure about 18˝ × 22˝ and often come precut. If you can't find precut fat quarters at your fabric shop you can always ask if they'll cut one for you at the cutting counter.

Yield: 1 sunglasses case

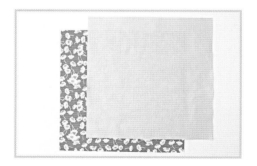

Prepare the following pieces:

OUTER—9˝ tall x 9˝ wide

LINING—9˝ tall x 9˝ wide

1

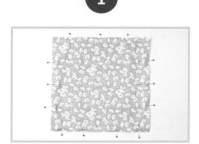

Step 1: Pin LINING to OUTER

With the LINING and OUTER right sides together, measure 3″ from each corner along the bottom edge and pin. The space between these two pins will mark where the opening will be when you sew. Continue pinning around the sunglasses case.

2

Step 2: Sew LINING to OUTER

Starting at one end of the opening, backstitch and sew around the sunglasses case using a ½″ seam allowance. Stop and backstitch at the other end of the opening.

3

Step 3: Clip corners

Snip off the corners of the sunglasses case, making sure not to cut through the stitching.

4

Step 4: Turn right side out and press

Turn the sunglasses case right side out.

Use a chopstick to gently push the corners into place.

Press the sunglasses case to keep the edges crisp. Keep the raw edges along the opening neatly tucked inside as you press.

5

Step 5: Edgestitch across top edge

With the OUTER facing up, edgestitch across the top edge of the sunglasses case, making sure to backstitch as you start and stop.

6

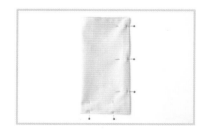

Step 6: Pin side and bottom

With the LINING facing up and the sewn edge at the top, fold the sunglasses case in half. The OUTER will now be showing and the LINING will be hidden inside.

Carefully align the sides and bottom of the case and pin in place. Be sure the opening along the bottom stays neat as you pin it.

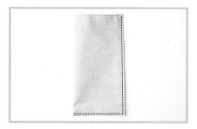

Step 7: Edgestitch side and bottom edges

Starting at the top right corner, edgestitch down the side and across the bottom of the sunglasses case, making sure to backstitch as you start and stop.

Finished!

KNOT HEADBAND

Tie this classic headband on for a fun and timeless look. Great for women and girls of all ages! Because the headband simply ties in place, the fit will always be perfect!

You will need:

- ¼ yard quilting cotton
- All-purpose thread

Yield: 1 headband

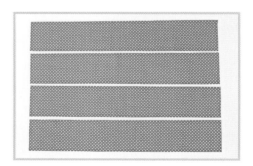

Prepare the following pieces:

Copy the KNOT HEADBAND TIP pattern piece on page 170 according to the instructions for copying patterns on page 10. Use the copied KNOT HEADBAND TIP pattern piece to trim the ends as directed in step 1.

Cut 4 rectangles measuring 3˝ tall x 18˝ wide

Step 1: Trim rectangle ends using pattern

Fold one rectangle in half lengthwise.

Align the KNOT HEADBAND TIP pattern piece (see page 170) along the fold at one end of the rectangle.

Cut along the curved line of the KNOT HEADBAND TIP pattern piece. (Do not cut the fabric across the bottom of the pattern piece.) Open the folded rectangle and iron to remove the crease.

Do this for each of the remaining rectangles. Be sure that you are only trimming one end of each rectangle. Keep the remaining end of each rectangle square.

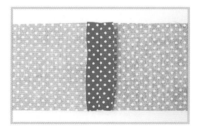

Step 4: Press seam allowance

Press the seam allowance open.

Repeat steps 2–4 to create the headband BACK from the remaining two pieces.

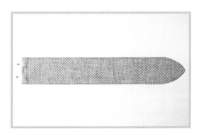

Step 2: Pin two pieces together

To create the front of the headband, pin two of the pieces together along the short (3″) edge with right sides together.

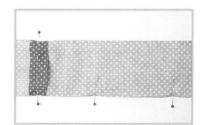

Step 5: Pin seam and opening

Place the FRONT on top of the BACK with the right sides together.

Pin the FRONT and BACK together on each side of the center seam.

Along the bottom edge of the headband, measure 3″ to the right of the center seam and pin. Then measure 7″ to the right of the center seam and pin. The space between these two pins will mark where the opening will be when you sew. Continue pinning around the headband.

Step 3: Sew pieces together

Sew the pieces together using a ½″ seam allowance. Be sure to backstitch as you start and stop. This will create the headband FRONT.

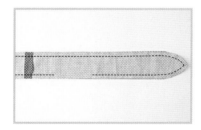

Step 6: Sew FRONT to BACK

Starting at one end of the opening, backstitch and sew all the way around the headband using a ½″ seam allowance. Stop and backstitch at the other end of the opening.

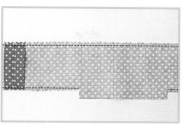

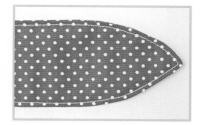

Step 7: Trim the seam allowance

Use pinking shears to trim the seam allowance to about ⅛″ all the way around the headband except across the opening. Do not trim the seam allowance across the opening.

Step 8: Turn right side out and press

Turn the headband right side out.

Use a chopstick to gently push the tips of the headband into place.

Press the headband to keep the edges crisp. Keep the raw edges along the opening neatly tucked inside as you press.

Pin the opening shut.

Step 9: Edgestitch around headband

Starting at the center seam, edgestitch all the way around the headband, making sure to backstitch as you start and stop.

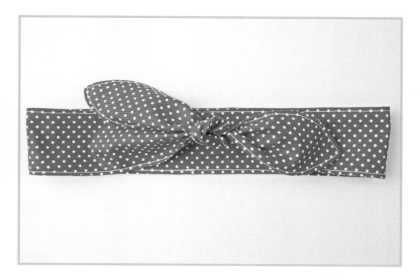

Finished!

To use:

Wrap the headband around your head.

Bring the tips of the headband together at the front.

Tie the ends into a square knot on top of your head.

SCRIPTURE BAG

With a handy front pocket and plenty of room for scriptures and a journal, this simple scripture bag is perfect for kids or adults.

Don't forget to add a little something inside your bag to snack on too!

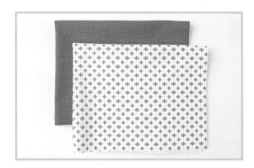

You will need:

- ⅓ yard quilting cotton for the OUTER and the STRAPS

- ⅓ yard quilting cotton for the LINING and the POCKET

- All-purpose thread

Yield: 1 scripture bag

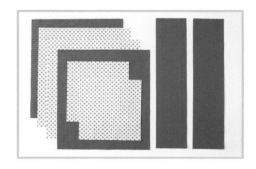

Prepare the following pieces:

OUTER FRONT and BACK—10˝ tall × 9˝ wide

LINING FRONT and BACK—10˝ tall × 9˝ wide

STRAPS—3˝ tall × 13˝ wide (cut 2 straps)

POCKET FRONT and BACK—6˝ tall × 6˝ wide

39

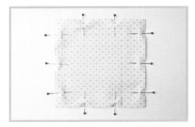

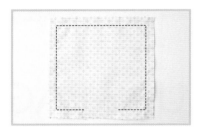

Step 1: Pin POCKET FRONT to POCKET BACK

With the POCKET FRONT and POCKET BACK right sides together, measure 2˝ from each corner along the bottom edge and pin. The space between these two pins will mark where the opening will be when you sew. Continue pinning around the POCKET.

Step 2: Sew POCKET FRONT to BACK

Starting at one end of the opening, backstitch and sew around the POCKET using a ½˝ seam allowance. Stop and backstitch at the other end of the opening.

Step 3: Clip POCKET corners

Snip off the corners of the POCKET, making sure not to cut through the stitching.

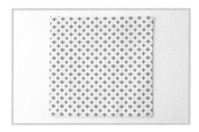

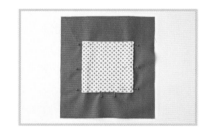

Step 4: Turn POCKET right side out and press

Turn the POCKET right side out.

Use a chopstick to gently push the corners into place.

Press the POCKET to keep the edges crisp. Keep the raw edges along the opening neatly tucked inside as you press.

Step 5: Edgestitch across top of POCKET

Edgestitch across the top edge of the POCKET, making sure to backstitch as you start and stop.

Step 6: Pin POCKET to OUTER FRONT

With the sewn edge of the pocket at the top, center the POCKET on top of the OUTER FRONT with the top edge of the POCKET 2½˝ away from the top edge of the OUTER FRONT and the sides of the POCKET 2˝ away from the sides of the OUTER FRONT.

Pin the POCKET in place along the bottom and sides of the POCKET.

Step 7: Sew POCKET to OUTER FRONT

Edgestitch along one side, across the bottom, and along the other side of the pocket, making sure to backstitch as you start and stop. Do not sew across the top edge of the pocket.

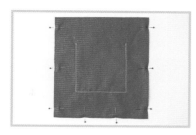

Step 8: Pin OUTER FRONT to BACK

Pin the OUTER FRONT to the BACK with the right sides together along the bottom and side edges.

Step 9: Sew FRONT to BACK

Sew along one side, across the bottom, and along the remaining side using a ½″ seam allowance, making sure to backstitch as you start and stop.

Step 10: Clip corners

Snip off the bottom corners of the OUTER, making sure not to cut through the stitching.

Step 11: Fold and press top edge

Fold the top edge over ½″ all the way around and press.

Step 12: Create LINING

Repeat steps 8–11 to create the LINING.

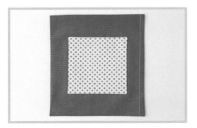

Step 13: Turn OUTER right side out and press

Turn the OUTER right side out.

Use a chopstick to gently push the corners into place.

Press the OUTER to keep the edges crisp. Keep the fold along the top edge neatly tucked inside as you press.

Do not turn the LINING right side out.

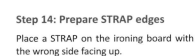

Step 14: Prepare STRAP edges

Place a STRAP on the ironing board with the wrong side facing up.

Fold each long (13″) edge over ½″ and press.

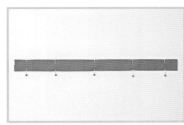

Step 15: Fold STRAP

Fold the entire STRAP in half lengthwise, making sure the folded edges from step 14 are aligned.

Press all the way along the new fold.

Pin the STRAP along the open edge.

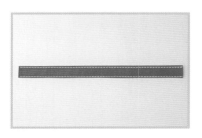

Step 16: Sew STRAP

Edgestitch along both long (13″) edges of the STRAP, making sure to backstitch as you start and stop.

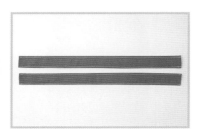

Step 17: Create remaining STRAP

Repeat steps 14–16 to create the remaining STRAP.

Step 18: Pin STRAP to OUTER FRONT

Unfold the top edge of the OUTER.

With the top of the STRAP facing down, position the outside edge of the strap 3″ from the side seam and pin in place on OUTER FRONT. Measure in 3″ from the opposite side seam and pin the remaining end of the STRAP in place.

As you pin, be sure to only pin through the OUTER FRONT. Do not pin through both layers of the OUTER.

Step 19: Sew STRAP to OUTER FRONT

Edgestitch along both ends of the STRAP, making sure to backstitch as you start and stop.

As you sew, be sure to only sew through the OUTER FRONT. Do not sew through both layers of the OUTER.

Repeat steps 18–19 to attach the remaining STRAP on the OUTER BACK.

Step 20: Refold and press top edge

With both straps sewn to the top edge of the OUTER, refold the top edge of the OUTER along the original ½″ fold line. The straps should now be sticking straight up out of the OUTER.

Press along the fold again to keep the top edge crisp.

Step 21: Pin LINING inside OUTER

Insert the LINING inside the OUTER. Match the side seams and the folded edge along the top of the OUTER and LINING and pin the LINING in place all the way around the bag opening.

Step 22: Edgestitch around opening

Start at a side seam and edgestitch around the entire opening of the bag, making sure to backstitch as you start and stop. The purpose of this edgestitching is to attach the LINING to the OUTER. Do not sew the opening shut.

Step 23: Topstitch around opening

Start at a side seam and topstitch around the entire opening of the bag ½″ from the top edge, making sure to backstitch as you start and stop. This extra row of stitching will add to the strength of your bag.

Finished!

43

Chapter Two

Home

REVERSIBLE PLACE MATS

It's always great to have a set of place mats on hand, and since these place mats are reversible, it's like making two sets at once! Use them to spruce up your everyday place settings or to keep kid messes at bay.

Bonus: these place mats are machine washable!

You will need:

- ½ yard quilting cotton for the FRONT
- ½ yard quilting cotton for the BACK
- All-purpose thread

Yield: 2 place mats

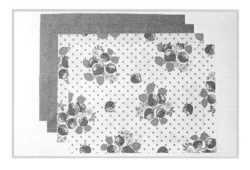

Prepare the following pieces:

FRONT —13˝ tall × 17˝ wide (cut 2 pieces)

BACK—13˝ tall × 17˝ wide (cut 2 pieces)

1

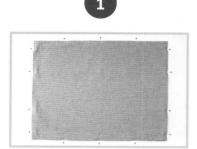

Step 1: Pin FRONT to BACK

With one of the FRONT pieces and one of the BACK pieces right sides together, measure 4″ from each corner along the right edge and pin. The space between these two pins will mark where the opening will be when you sew. Continue pinning around the place mat.

2

Step 2: Sew FRONT to BACK

Starting at one end of the opening, backstitch and sew around the place mat using a ½″ seam allowance. Stop and backstitch at the other end of the opening.

3

Step 3: Clip corners

Snip off the corners of the place mat, making sure not to cut through the stitching.

4

Step 4: Turn place mat right side out and press

Turn the place mat right side out.

Use a chopstick to gently push the corners into place.

Press the place mat to keep the edges crisp. Keep the raw edges along the opening neatly tucked inside as you press.

Pin the opening shut.

5

Step 5: Edgestitch around place mat

Edgestitch around the place mat, making sure to backstitch as you start and stop.

6

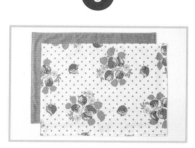

Step 6: Create remaining place mat

Repeat steps 1–5 to create the second place mat from the remaining FRONT and BACK pieces.

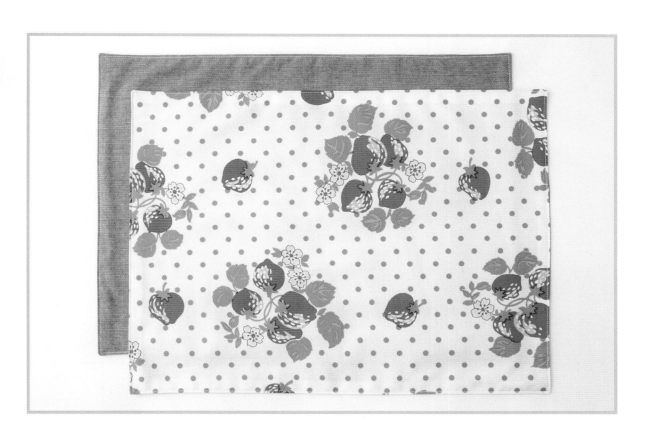

Finished!

FABRIC BASKET

This fabric basket is great for organizing your drawers or desktop.

It's collapsible, reversible, and so quick and easy to make!

You will need:

- ⅓ yard quilting cotton for the FRONT
- ⅓ yard quilting cotton for the BACK
- ⅓ yard felt for the LINING
- 2 yards ½″-wide twill tape for the TIES
- All-purpose thread

TIP: If you don't want to buy the full ⅓ yard of fabric for the FRONT or BACK, buy 1 fat quarter for each instead. Fat quarters of fabric typically measure about 18″ × 22″ and often come precut. If you can't find precut fat quarters at your fabric shop you can always ask if they'll cut one for you at the cutting counter.

Yield: 1 fabric basket

Prepare the following pieces:

FRONT—11″ tall × 11″ wide

BACK—11″ tall × 11″ wide

LINING—11″ tall × 11″ wide

TIES—cut 8 ties measuring 8″ long

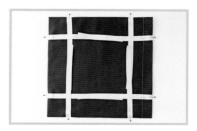

Step 1: Pin TIES to BACK and LINING

Place the BACK right side up on top of the LINING, matching the edges.

Pin one end of each TIE in place 2″ away from each corner.

Position the remaining loose end of each TIE in toward the middle of the fabric basket so it won't get caught as you sew.

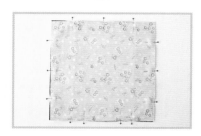

Step 2: Pin FRONT to BACK

Place the FRONT right side down on top of the TIES, BACK and LINING, matching the edges.

Measure 3½″ from each corner along the bottom edge and pin. The space between these two pins will mark where the opening will be when you sew. Remove one of the TIE pins, and replace it with the pin going through all four layers. Replace all of the TIE pins in this way, working one at a time.

Continue pinning as needed.

Step 3: Sew FRONT to TIES, BACK, and LINING

Starting at one end of the opening, backstitch and sew around the fabric basket using a ½″ seam allowance. Stop and backstitch at the other end of the opening.

Step 4: Clip corners

Snip off the corners of the fabric basket, making sure not to cut through the stitching.

Step 5: Trim LINING

Turn the fabric basket over so the LINING is facing up. Trim the seam allowance of the LINING to ⅛″ along all sides.

Step 6: Turn basket right side out and press

Turn the fabric basket right side out.

Use a chopstick to gently push the corners into place. Press the fabric basket to keep the edges crisp. Keep the raw edges along the opening neatly tucked inside as you press.

Pin the opening shut.

Step 7: Edgestitch around basket

Starting at the bottom right corner, edge-stitch around the fabric basket, making sure to backstitch as you start and stop.

Step 8: Tie TIES

To form the fabric basket, tie the TIES next to each corner together into a bow. As you pull the TIES tight to form the bow, the corners of the basket will come together, giving the basket its shape.

Finished!

MICROWAVE HEAT PACK

In our house, we love to keep a few of these heat packs around to keep our toes warm on chilly nights. Just heat one up in the microwave 1–2 minutes, tuck it under the covers before crawling into bed, and it will keep you toasty warm while you fall asleep. This heat pack is also great for soothing aches and pains.

You will need:

- ¼ yard flannel for the FRONT and the BACK

- 1½ cups uncooked rice

- All-purpose thread

TIP: If you don't want to buy the full ¼ yard of fabric, just buy 1 fat quarter instead. Fat quarters of fabric typically measure about 18″ × 22″ and often come precut. If you can't find precut fat quarters at your fabric shop you can always ask if they'll cut one for you at the cutting counter.

Yield: 1 heat pack

Prepare the following pieces:

FRONT—5″ tall × 10″ wide

BACK—5″ tall × 10″ wide

1

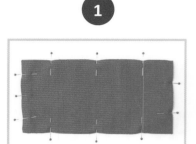

Step 1: Pin FRONT to BACK

With the FRONT and BACK right sides together, measure 1½˝ from each corner along the right edge and pin. The space between these two pins will mark where the opening will be when you sew. Continue pinning around the heat pack.

2

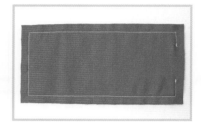

Step 2: Sew FRONT to BACK

Starting at one end of the opening, backstitch and sew around the heat pack using a ½˝ seam allowance. Stop and backstitch at the other end of the opening.

3

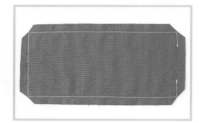

Step 3: Clip corners

Snip off the corners of the heat pack, making sure not to cut through the stitching.

4

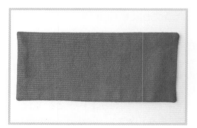

Step 4: Turn heat pack right side out and press

Turn the heat pack right side out.

Use a chopstick to gently push the corners into place. Press the heat pack to keep the edges crisp. Keep the raw edges along the opening neatly tucked inside as you press.

5

Step 5: Edgestitch along bottom, left side, and top

Edgestitch across the bottom, along the left side, and across the top of the heat pack, making sure to backstitch as you start and stop. Do not edgestitch along the right side or you will close the opening.

6

Step 6: Fill heat pack with rice

Fill the heat pack with 1½ cups uncooked rice.

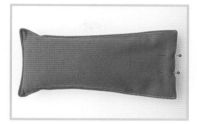

Step 7: Pin opening

Pin the opening shut. See the instructions on page 9 for inserting pins into stuffed items. As you pin, be sure to keep the rice well away from the right edge.

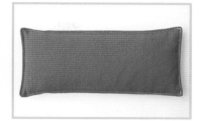

Step 8: Edgestitch along right edge

Edgestitch along the right edge, making sure to backstitch as you start and stop. Be sure to keep the rice away from the right edge as you sew.

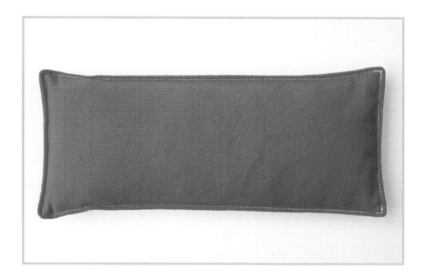

Finished!

To use: Warm up the heat pack in the microwave for 1–2 minutes.

PILLOW PINCUSHION

Every seamstress needs a place to keep her pins. This fun little pincushion will help keep your sewing room tidy and look great doing it.

You will need:

- ¼ yard quilting cotton for the FRONT
- ¼ yard quilting cotton for the BACK
- Stuffing
- ½˝ button
- All-purpose thread

TIP: If you don't want to buy the full ¼ yard of fabric for the FRONT or BACK, buy 1 fat quarter for each instead. Fat quarters of fabric typically measure about 18˝ × 22˝ and often come precut. If you can't find precut fat quarters at your fabric shop you can always ask if they'll cut one for you at the cutting counter.

Yield: 1 pincushion

Prepare the following pieces:

FRONT—6˝ tall × 6˝ wide

BACK—6˝ tall × 6˝ wide

1

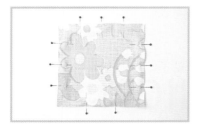

2

3

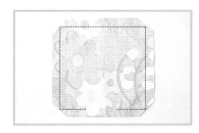

Step 1: Pin FRONT to BACK

With the FRONT and BACK right sides together, measure 2˝ from each corner along the bottom edge and pin. The space between these two pins will mark where the opening will be when you sew. Continue pinning around the pincushion.

Step 2: Sew FRONT to BACK

Starting at one end of the opening, backstitch and sew around the pincushion using a ½˝ seam allowance. Stop and backstitch at the other end of the opening.

Step 3: Clip corners

Snip off the corners of the pincushion, making sure not to cut through the stitching.

4

5

6

Step 4: Turn pincushion right side out and press

Turn the pincushion right side out.

Use a chopstick to gently push the corners into place. Press the pincushion to keep the edges crisp. Keep the raw edges along the opening neatly tucked inside as you press.

Step 5: Edgestitch along top and sides

Starting at the bottom left corner, edgestitch along the left side, across the top, and along the right side of the pincushion. Do not edgestitch across the bottom edge.

Step 6: Fill pincushion with stuffing

Fill the pincushion with stuffing until the pincushion is about 1½˝ tall at the center.

Step 7: Pin opening

Push the stuffing away from the open end and pin the opening shut. See the instructions on page 9 for inserting pins into stuffed items.

Step 8: Edgestitch across bottom edge

Edgestitch across the bottom edge, making sure to backstitch as you start and stop. Be sure to keep the stuffing away from the bottom edge as you sew.

Step 9: Stitch through pincushion

Distribute the stuffing evenly throughout the pincushion.

Use your fingers to push the stuffing away from the center of the pincushion.

Cut an arm's length of thread and thread it onto a hand-sewing needle. Move the needle to the center of the thread to create a double layer of thread. Tie the thread ends together into a knot.

With the FRONT of the pincushion facing up, insert the needle down through the center of the pincushion and gently pull until the knot is flush with the top of the pincushion. Insert the needle back up through the center of the pincushion about ⅛″ away from the previous stitch. Pull the thread all the way back up through the pincushion, gently pulling the thread tight so the top and bottom of the pincushion come together and touch at the center.

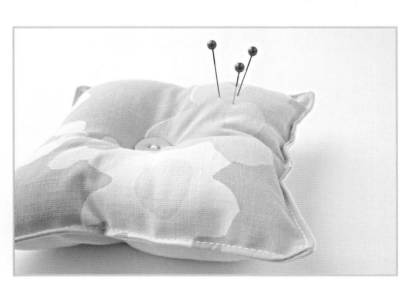

Finished!

Step 10: Sew button

Add the button to the center of the pincushion and sew it in place. See the instructions for how to sew on a button on page 12.

TRAVEL PILLOW & PILLOWCASE

Whether you're traveling by car, train, or plane, this cozy travel pillow will keep you comfortable and cozy. About half the size of a regular pillow, it's just the right size for travel. And unlike most travel pillows, this one has a pillowcase that can be thrown in the wash when you get home.

You will need:

- ⅓ yard quilting cotton for the PILLOW
- ½ yard quilting cotton for the PILLOWCASE OUTER
- ½ yard quilting cotton for the PILLOWCASE LINING
- Stuffing
- All-purpose thread

Yield: 1 travel pillow & pillowcase

Prepare the following pieces:

PILLOW FRONT and BACK—12″ tall × 18″ wide

PILLOWCASE OUTER FRONT and BACK—13″ tall × 21″ wide

PILLOWCASE LINING FRONT and BACK—13″ tall × 21″ wide

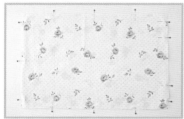

Step 1: Pin PILLOW FRONT to BACK

With the PILLOW FRONT and BACK right sides together, measure 3″ from each corner along the right edge and pin. The space between these two pins will mark where the opening will be when you sew. Continue pinning around the pillow.

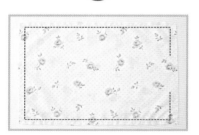

Step 2: Sew PILLOW FRONT to PILLOW BACK

Starting at one end of the opening, backstitch and sew around the pillow using a ½″ seam allowance. Stop and backstitch at the other end of the opening.

Step 3: Clip corners

Snip off the corners of the pillow, making sure not to cut through the stitching.

Step 4: Turn pillow right side out and press

Turn the pillow right side out.

Use a chopstick to gently push the corners into place. Press the pillow to keep the edges crisp. Keep the raw edges along the opening neatly tucked inside as you press.

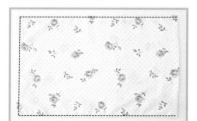

Step 5: Edgestitch along bottom, left side, and top

With the FRONT of the pillow facing up, start at the bottom right corner and edgestitch across the bottom, along the left side, and across the top of the pillow. Do not edgestitch across the right edge.

Step 6: Fill pillow with stuffing

Fill the pillow with stuffing until the pillow is about 4″ tall at the center.

Step 7: Pin opening

Push the stuffing away from the open end and pin the opening shut. See the instructions on page 9 for inserting pins into stuffed items.

Step 8: Edgestitch along right edge

Edgestitch along the right edge, making sure to backstitch as you start and stop. Be sure to keep the stuffing away from the right edge as you sew. The pillow is now finished.

Step 9: Pin PILLOWCASE OUTER FRONT to BACK

With the PILLOWCASE OUTER FRONT and BACK right sides together, pin along the top, bottom, and left edge of the pillowcase OUTER. Do not pin along the right edge.

Step 10: Sew FRONT to BACK

Sew across the bottom, along the left side, and across the top of the pillowcase using a ½″ seam allowance, making sure to backstitch as you start and stop.

Step 11: Fold and press opening

Fold the open edge over ½″ and press.

Step 12: Clip corners

Snip off the remaining corners of the pillowcase OUTER, making sure not to cut through the stitching.

13

Step 13: Create PILLOWCASE LINING

Repeat steps 9–12 to create the PILLOWCASE LINING.

14

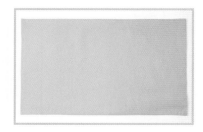

Step 14: Turn PILLOWCASE OUTER right side out and press

Turn the PILLOWCASE OUTER right side out.

Use a chopstick to gently push the corners into place. Press the PILLOWCASE OUTER to keep the edges crisp. Keep the fold along the opening neatly tucked inside as you press.

Do not turn the PILLOWCASE LINING right side out.

15

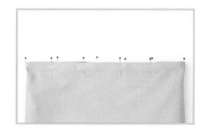

Step 15: Pin PILLOWCASE LINING inside PILLOWCASE OUTER

Insert the PILLOWCASE LINING into the PILLOWCASE OUTER. Match the side seams and the fold along the opening and pin in place all the way around the opening.

16

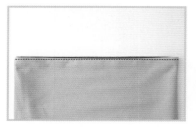

Step 16: Edgestitch around pillowcase opening

Start at a side seam and edgestitch around the entire opening of the pillowcase, making sure to backstitch as you start and stop. The purpose of this edgestitching is to attach the PILLOWCASE LINING to the PILLOWCASE OUTER. Do not sew the opening shut.

17

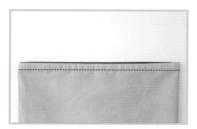

Step 17: Topstitch along pillowcase opening

Start at a side seam and topstitch around the entire opening of the pillowcase ½″ away from the edge of the pillowcase opening, making sure to backstitch as you start and stop. This extra row of stitching will add to the strength of your pillowcase.

Finished!

Insert the pillow into the pillowcase and you're all set for your next big trip!

Chapter Three

Celebrations

SCRAP FLAG GARLAND

Draping a freshly made garland is sure to add cheer to all of your festivities! This fun scrap flag garland is a great way to use up and showcase some of your favorite scraps from your fabric stash. And it's so fast and easy to put together—you'll be ready to party in no time!

You will need:

- ⅛ yard quilting cotton or assorted fabric scraps for the FLAGS

- 3 yards cotton yarn for the STRING

- All-purpose thread

Yield: 1 garland

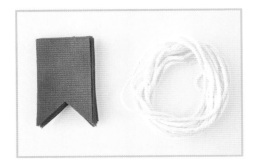

Prepare the following pieces:

Copy the SCRAP FLAG GARLAND pattern piece on page 170 according to the instructions for copying patterns on page 10. Use the copied SCRAP FLAG GARLAND pattern piece to cut the following pieces from fabric.

FLAGS—Cut 22 flags from the SCRAP FLAG GARLAND pattern piece

STRING—Cut a piece of yarn 3 yards long

Step 1: Fold top edges of FLAGS

With the wrong side of the flag facing up, fold the top edge over ½″ and press.

Do this for all 22 flags.

Step 2: Pin first FLAG to STRING

Position the first FLAG so the left edge of the flag is 11¼″ from the end of the STRING.

Tuck the STRING up inside the fold of the FLAG and pin it in place.

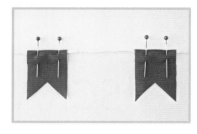

Step 3: Pin remaining FLAGS to STRING

Pin the remaining 21 FLAGS onto the STRING with 2½″ of STRING in between each flag.

Tuck the STRING up inside the fold of each FLAG and pin in place.

There will be 11¼″ of STRING left at the opposite end of the garland.

Step 4: Sew FLAGS onto STRING.

Edgestitch across the top fold on each FLAG, making sure to backstitch as you start and stop.

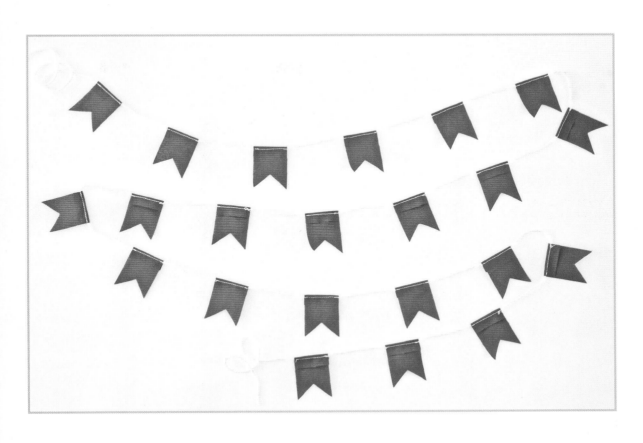

Finished!

TOOTH FAIRY PILLOW

Celebrate each lost tooth with this fun tooth fairy pillow!

Just tuck the lost tooth inside the front pocket of the pillow for safekeeping.

Kids will love hiding this little pillow under their big pillow at night and

waking up in the morning to find a new treasure in the pocket!

You will need:

- ¼ yard quilting cotton for the PILLOW

- ¼ yard quilting cotton for the POCKET

- Stuffing

- All-purpose thread

TIP: If you don't want to buy the full ¼ yard of fabric for the pillow or pocket, buy 1 fat quarter for each instead. Fat quarters of fabric typically measure about 18″ × 22″ and often come precut. If you can't find precut fat quarters at your fabric shop you can always ask if they'll cut one for you at the cutting counter.

Yield: 1 tooth fairy pillow

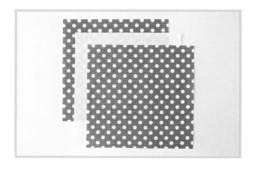

Prepare the following pieces:

PILLOW FRONT and BACK—5″ tall × 5″ wide

POCKET—5″ tall × 5″ wide

Step 1: Fold POCKET

Fold the POCKET in half with the wrong sides together.

Press the fold.

Step 2: Edgestitch along fold of POCKET

Edgestitch along the fold of the pocket, making sure to backstitch as you start and stop.

Step 3: Pin POCKET to PILLOW FRONT

Align the bottom and side edges of the POCKET with the bottom and side edges of the PILLOW FRONT. Pin the POCKET in place at the top edge.

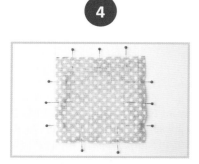

Step 4: Pin PILLOW FRONT to BACK

With the PILLOW FRONT and BACK right sides together, measure 1½″ from each corner along the bottom edge and pin. The space between these two pins will mark where the opening will be when you sew. Continue pinning around the remaining edges.

As you pin, remove each of the pins from step 3 and replace them with pins going through all three layers. The POCKET will now be sandwiched in between the PILLOW FRONT and BACK.

Step 5: Sew PILLOW FRONT to BACK

Starting at one end of the opening, backstitch and sew around the pillow using a ½″ seam allowance. Stop and backstitch at the other end of the opening.

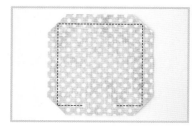

Step 6: Clip corners

Snip off the corners of the pillow, making sure not to cut through the stitching.

7

Step 7: Turn pillow right side out and press

Turn the pillow right side out.

Use a chopstick to gently push the corners into place. Press the pillow to keep the edges crisp. Keep the raw edges along the opening neatly tucked inside as you press.

8

Step 8: Edgestitch along sides and top

Edgestitch along the left side, across the top, and along the remaining side of the pillow. Do not edgestitch across the bottom edge.

9

Step 9: Fill pillow with stuffing

Fill the pillow with stuffing until it is about 1″ tall at the center.

10

Step 10: Pin opening

Push the stuffing away from the open end and pin the opening shut. See the instructions on page 9 for inserting pins into stuffed items.

11

Step 11: Edgestitch along bottom edge

Edgestitch along the bottom edge, making sure to backstitch as you start and stop. Be sure to keep the stuffing away from the bottom edge as you sew.

Finished!

POM-POM GARLAND

This whimsical pom-pom garland

will add an element of fun to your holiday and party decorations.

And it takes just minutes to make!

You will need:

- 52 pom-poms, ½˝ size
- All-purpose thread for the STRING

Yield: 1 pom-pom garland

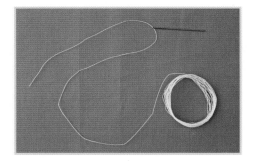

Prepare the following pieces:

STRING—Cut a piece of thread 3 yards long

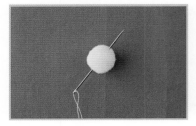

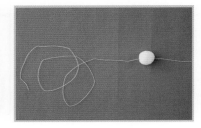

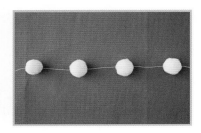

Step 1: Add first pom-pom

Thread the STRING onto your hand-sewing needle.

Do not tie any knots.

Poke the needle through the center of a pom-pom.

Step 2: Position first pom-pom on STRING

Slide the first pom-pom down the STRING until the pom-pom is 15½˝ from the end of the STRING.

You do not need to tie any knots. The pom-pom will stay in place. However, if you want the pom pom to stay permanently in place so it won't move when pulled, add a small dot of hot glue to the end of the pom pom where the string enters it.

Step 3: Add remaining pom-poms to STRING

Add the remaining 51 pom-poms to the STRING with 1˝ of STRING in between each pom-pom.

There will be 15½˝ of STRING left at the opposite end of the garland.

Once all of the pom-poms are in place on the STRING, remove the needle.

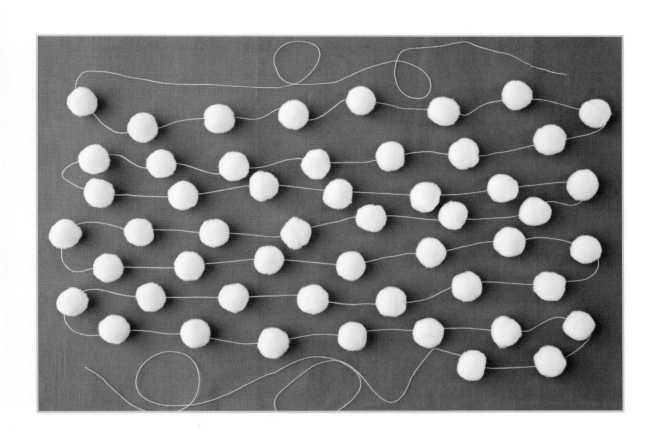

Finished!

STOCKING

Coming down the stairs on Christmas morning to a stocking full of surprises has always been a favorite Christmas tradition in our home. This timeless stocking is so simple to put together and just the right size for filling with all of your favorite Christmas goodies. Make one for every member of the family!

You will need:

- ⅓ yard quilting cotton for the OUTER
- ⅓ yard quilting cotton for the LINING
- 7″ of ½″-wide twill tape for the HANGING LOOP
- All-purpose thread

Yield: 1 stocking

Prepare the following pieces:

Copy and assemble the 5 parts of the STOCKING pattern on pages 171–175 to create the complete STOCKING pattern. To copy the pattern pieces, follow the instructions for copying patterns on page 10. Use the assembled STOCKING pattern to cut the following pieces from fabric.

OUTER FRONT and BACK—cut from the STOCKING pattern piece

LINING FRONT and BACK — cut from the STOCKING pattern piece

HANGING LOOP—cut a 7″ long piece of ½″-wide twill tape

Note: If you are using fabric with a right side and a wrong side, fold the fabric in half, right sides together, and then cut both the OUTER FRONT and OUTER BACK pieces at once. This will ensure that you don't end up with two FRONTs or two BACKs. Do the same for the LINING pieces if necessary.

1

Step 1: Pin OUTER FRONT to BACK

Pin the OUTER FRONT to the BACK with the right sides together. Do not pin across the top.

2

Step 2: Sew FRONT to BACK

Sew all the way around the stocking using a ½˝ seam allowance, except across the top. Do not sew across the top. Be sure to backstitch as you start and stop sewing.

3

Step 3: Trim seam allowance

Use pinking shears to trim the seam allowance to about ⅛˝ all the way around the OUTER except across the top. As you trim, make sure not to cut through the stitching.

4

Step 4: Fold and press top edge

Fold the top edge over ½˝ all the way around and press.

5

Step 5: Create LINING

Repeat steps 1–4 to create the LINING.

6

Step 6: Turn OUTER right side out and press

Turn the OUTER right side out.

Use a chopstick to gently push the curves into place.

Press the OUTER to keep the edges crisp. Keep the fold along the top edge neatly tucked inside as you press.

Do not turn the LINING right side out.

Step 7: Pin LINING inside OUTER

Insert the LINING inside the OUTER. Match the side seams and the folded edge along the top of the stocking and pin in place all the way around the opening.

Step 8: Edgestitch around opening

Start at the side seam along the back edge of the stocking and edgestitch around the entire opening of the stocking, making sure to backstitch as you start and stop. The purpose of this edgestitching is to attach the LINING to the OUTER. Do not sew the opening shut.

Step 9: Fold cuff into place

Fold the top of the stocking over by 4″ all the way around the stocking to form the cuff.

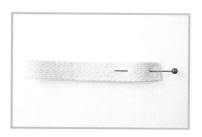

Step 10: Pin HANGING LOOP

With the right sides together, fold the twill tape in half to create the HANGING LOOP. Align the raw ends, and pin the ends together.

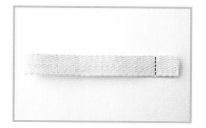

Step 11: Sew HANGING LOOP

Sew the ends of the HANGING LOOP together using a ½″ seam allowance. Be sure to backstitch as you start and stop.

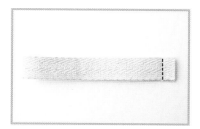

Step 12: Trim seam allowance

Trim the seam allowance on the HANGING LOOP to ¼″.

Step 13: Turn HANGING LOOP right side out and press

Turn the HANGING LOOP right side out. The seam allowance will now be sandwiched in between the two layers of the HANGING LOOP. Press the HANGING LOOP to keep the folded ends crisp.

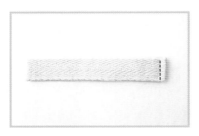

Step 14: Edgestitch across HANGING LOOP

Edgestitch across the sewn end of the HANGING LOOP, making sure to backstitch as you start and stop.

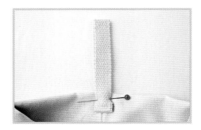

Step 15: Pin HANGING LOOP to stocking

Inside the stocking, center the bottom (sewn) edge of the HANGING LOOP over the seam at the back edge of the stocking and down ½″ from the edge of the fold at the top of the stocking.

Pin the HANGING LOOP in place.

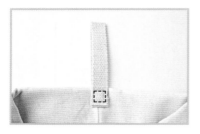

Step 16: Sew HANGING LOOP onto stocking

To attach the HANGING LOOP to the stocking, sew a small square at the bottom of the HANGING LOOP. To do this, edgestitch across the existing line of stitching on the bottom of the HANGING LOOP, up one of the sides for about ½″, across the HANGING LOOP, and down the opposite side of the HANGING LOOP, making sure to backstitch as you start and stop. Sew around the square twice to reinforce the stitching.

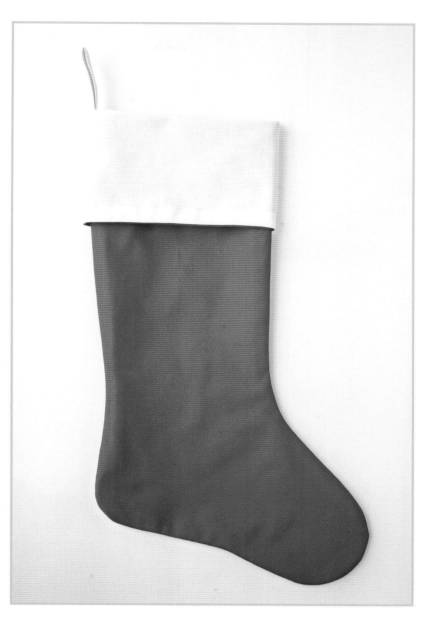

Finished!

FELT NATIVITY PUPPETS

Kids will love acting out the Christmas story with these fun nativity puppets. They're soft, quiet, and they store flat, making them a great addition to your quiet bag for church. Or pull them out on Christmas Eve and put on a family puppet show! Just poke your fingers up inside the puppets to bring them to life. You can make a lot of the other characters from the nativity story from these basic patterns and instructions too. Use the Joseph pattern and change the colors of the robe and head covering to make the three wise men or shepherds. Use the Mary pattern and add wings for an angel. So many possibilities!

You will need:

- 1 sheet of dark green felt for the JOSEPH FRONT and BACK

- 1 sheet of light green felt for the JOSEPH HEAD COVERING FRONT and BACK

- 1 sheet of brown felt for the JOSEPH BEARD

- 1 sheet of dark blue felt for the MARY FRONT and BACK

- 1 sheet of light blue felt for the MARY HEAD COVERING FRONT and BACK

- 1 sheet of white felt for the BABY JESUS FRONT and BACK

- 1 sheet of red felt for the BABY JESUS BLANKET

- 1 sheet of beige felt for the JOSEPH, MARY, and BABY JESUS FACES

- All-purpose thread

Yield: 1 Joseph puppet, 1 Mary puppet, and 1 baby Jesus puppet

Prepare the following pieces:

Copy the Nativity pattern pieces on pages 176–178 according to the instructions for copying patterns on page 10. Use the copied Nativity pattern pieces to cut the following pieces from felt.

JOSEPH FRONT and BACK—cut 2 pieces

JOSEPH HEAD COVERING FRONT—cut 1 piece

JOSEPH HEAD COVERING BACK—cut 1 piece

JOSEPH/MARY FACE—cut 2 pieces

JOSEPH BEARD—cut 1 piece

MARY FRONT and BACK—cut 2 pieces

MARY HEAD COVERING FRONT—cut 1 piece

MARY HEAD COVERING BACK—cut 1 piece

BABY JESUS FRONT and BACK—cut 2 pieces

BABY JESUS BLANKET—cut 1 piece

BABY JESUS FACE—cut 1 piece

Step 1: Edgestitch along bottom of JOSEPH and MARY FRONT and BACK pieces

Edgestitch along the bottom edge of each of the FRONT and BACK pieces for JOSEPH and MARY, making sure to backstitch as you start and stop. This will stabilize the bottom edge of the puppets and help prevent them from becoming stretched during use.

Step 2: Pin HEAD COVERING pieces to FRONT and BACK pieces

Match the top edge of the JOSEPH HEAD COVERING FRONT to the top edge of the JOSEPH FRONT and pin in place along the bottom edge of the HEAD COVERING.

Repeat for the remaining HEAD COVERING pieces for the JOSEPH BACK and MARY FRONT and BACK pieces.

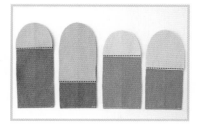

Step 3: Sew HEAD COVERING pieces to FRONT and BACK pieces

Edgestitch along the bottom edge of each of the HEAD COVERING pieces for JOSEPH and MARY, making sure to backstitch as you start and stop.

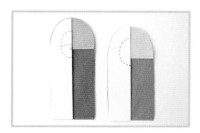

Step 4: Prep pattern pieces

Fold the JOSEPH FRONT and BACK pattern piece in half lengthwise and place it on top of the JOSEPH FRONT with the edges aligned.

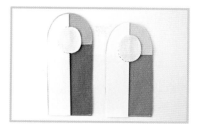

Step 5: Position FACES

Using the pattern as a guide, place the JOSEPH FACE on top of the JOSEPH FRONT.

Do the same to place the MARY FACE on top of the MARY FRONT.

Step 6: Pin FACES

Carefully remove the pattern pieces and pin the FACES in place.

Step 7: Sew FACES

Starting at the bottom of the JOSEPH FACE, edgestitch around the entire FACE, making sure to backstitch as you start and stop. When edgestitching around the FACE, go slowly and use the hand wheel.

Do the same for the MARY FACE.

Step 8: Pin BEARD

Place the BEARD on top of the JOSEPH FACE with the bottom edges aligned.

Pin the BEARD in place.

Step 9: Sew BEARD

Starting at one corner of the BEARD, edgestitch around the outside edge of the BEARD, making sure to backstitch as you start and stop. When edgestitching around the BEARD, go slowly and use the hand wheel.

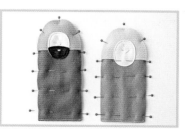

Step 10: Pin FRONTS to BACKS

Pin the JOSEPH FRONT to the JOSEPH BACK along the edges of the puppet with the wrong sides together. Do not pin across the bottom edge.

Do the same for the MARY FRONT and BACK.

Step 11: Sew FRONTS to BACKS

Starting at the bottom of the JOSEPH puppet, edgestitch along one side, around the top, and along the remaining side of the puppet, making sure to backstitch as you start and stop. Do not edgestitch across the bottom. When edgestitching around the curve at the top of the body, go slowly and use the hand wheel.

Do the same for the MARY puppet.

The JOSEPH and MARY puppets are now finished.

Step 12: Pin BABY JESUS BLANKET to FRONT

Match the bottom edge of the BABY JESUS BLANKET to the bottom edge of the BABY JESUS FRONT and pin the BLANKET to the FRONT along the top edge of the BLANKET.

Step 13: Edgestitch around BLANKET

Edgestitch around the entire BLANKET, making sure to backstitch as you start and stop. When edgestitching around the curves of the BLANKET, go slowly and use the hand wheel.

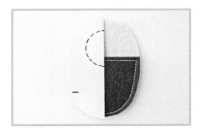

Step 14: Prep pattern piece

Fold the BABY JESUS FRONT and BACK pattern piece in half lengthwise and place it on top of the BABY JESUS FRONT with the edges aligned.

Step 15: Position FACE

Using the pattern as a guide, place the BABY JESUS FACE on top of the BABY JESUS FRONT.

Step 16: Pin FACE

Carefully remove the pattern piece and pin the FACE in place.

Step 17: Sew FACE

Starting at the bottom of the BABY JESUS FACE, edgestitch around the entire FACE, making sure to backstitch as you start and stop. When edgestitching around the FACE, go slowly and use the hand wheel.

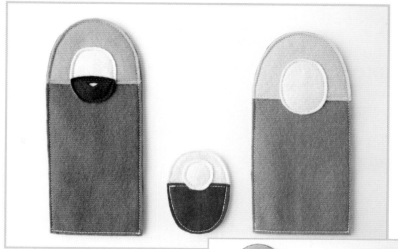

Finished!

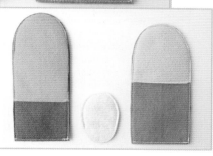

BACK VIEW

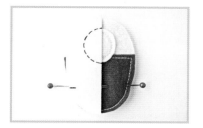

Step 18: Pin FRONT to BACK at opening

Pin the BABY JESUS FRONT to the BACK with the wrong sides together at the opening marked on the pattern piece. Do this for both the left and the right side of the puppet.

Step 19: Continue pinning FRONT to BACK

Continue pinning the FRONT to the BACK along the top and side edges of the puppet. Do not pin across the bottom of the puppet.

Step 20: Sew FRONT to BACK

Starting at one end of the opening, edgestitch along one side, around the top, and along the remaining side of the puppet, making sure to backstitch as you start and stop. Do not edgestitch across the bottom. When edgestitching around the curves of the body, go slowly and use the hand wheel.

Chapter Four

Baby

REVERSIBLE BIB

This simple, reversible bib is the perfect size for babies just starting to eat real food or for toddlers who love to feed themselves. It's big enough to cover them up all the way down to their tummies, so the food stays on the bib and off their clothes. Just throw it in the wash when it's dirty and it'll be good as new.

You will need:

- ⅓ yard quilting cotton for the FRONT
- ⅓ yard quilting cotton for the BACK
- 1″ of ¾″-wide Velcro
- All-purpose thread

TIP: If you don't want to buy the full ⅓ yard of fabric for the FRONT or BACK, buy 1 fat quarter for each instead. Fat quarters of fabric typically measure about 18″ × 22″ and often come precut. If you can't find precut fat quarters at your fabric shop you can always ask if they'll cut one for you at the cutting counter.

Yield: 1 bib

Prepare the following pieces:

Copy and assemble the 2 parts of the REVERSIBLE BIB pattern on pages 179–180 to create the complete REVERSIBLE BIB pattern. To copy the pattern pieces, follow the instructions for copying patterns on page 10. Use the assembled REVERSIBLE BIB pattern to cut the following pieces from fabric.

FRONT—cut from REVERSIBLE BIB pattern piece on fold

BACK— cut from REVERSIBLE BIB pattern piece on fold

Velcro—cut a 1″ piece

While the FRONT and BACK are still folded in half from cutting and the pattern is still in place, make a small snip at the line on the bottom of the pattern to the mark where the opening will be when you sew.

1

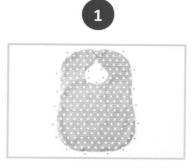

2

3

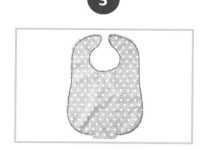

Step 1: Pin FRONT to BACK

With the FRONT and BACK right sides together, insert a pin at each snip along the bottom edge. The space between these two pins will mark where the opening will be when you sew. Continue pinning around the bib.

Step 2: Sew FRONT to BACK

Starting at one end of the opening, backstitch and sew around the bib using a ½″ seam allowance. Stop and backstitch at the other end of the opening. Go slow and use the hand wheel when sewing any tight curves.

Step 3: Trim seam allowance

Use pinking shears to trim the seam allowance to about ⅛″ all the way around the bib except across the opening at the bottom. Do not trim the opening along the bottom. As you trim, make sure not to cut through the stitching.

4

5

6

Step 4: Turn bib right side out and press

Turn the bib right side out.

Use a chopstick to gently push the curves into place.

Press the bib to keep the edges crisp. Keep the raw edges along the opening neatly tucked inside as you press.

Pin the opening shut.

Step 5: Edgestitch around bib

Starting at the tip of the tab on the right, edgestitch around the entire bib, making sure to backstitch as you start and stop.

Step 6: Pin hook side of Velcro onto bib

Peel the two pieces of Velcro apart so the hook side (scratchy) and the loop side (soft) are separate.

Center the hook side of the Velcro over the left tab on the bib, about ½″ away from the tip of the tab, and pin in place.

Step 7: Sew hook side of Velcro onto bib

Edgestitch all the way around the Velcro twice, making sure to backstitch as you start and stop.

Sew an X through the middle of the Velcro.

Step 8: Pin the loop side of Velcro onto bib

Turn the bib over so the BACK is facing up.

Center the loop side of the Velcro over the left tab on the bib, about a ½″ away from the tip of the tab, and pin in place.

Step 9: Sew the loop side of Velcro onto bib

Edgestitch all the way around the Velcro twice, making sure to backstitch as you start and stop.

Sew an X through the middle of the Velcro.

Finished!

BURP CLOTHS

A set of good, soft burp cloths is a necessity for every new baby. And they're not just for cleaning spit-up. Since these flannel burp cloths get softer with every wash, they're perfect for wiping runny noses too. Going to a baby shower? A fresh stack of burp cloths makes a great gift!

You will need:

- ½ yard flannel for the FRONT pieces
- ½ yard flannel for the BACK pieces
- All-purpose thread

Yield: 4 burp cloths

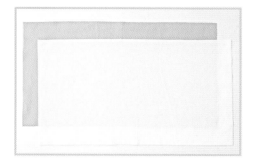

Prepare the following pieces:

FRONT—10″ tall × 18″ wide (cut 4 pieces)

BACK—10″ tall × 18″ wide (cut 4 pieces)

Step 1: Pin FRONT to BACK

With one of the FRONT pieces and one of the BACK pieces right sides together, measure 3˝ from each corner along the right edge and pin. The space between these two pins will mark where the opening will be when you sew. Continue pinning around the burp cloth.

Step 2: Sew FRONT to BACK

Starting at one end of the opening, backstitch and sew around the burp cloth using a ½˝ seam allowance. Stop and backstitch at the other end of the opening.

Step 3: Clip corners

Snip off the corners of the burp cloth, making sure not to cut through the stitching.

Step 4: Turn burp cloth right side out and press

Turn the burp cloth right side out.

Use a chopstick to gently push the corners into place. Press the burp cloth to keep the edges crisp. Keep the raw edges along the opening neatly tucked inside as you press.

Pin the opening shut.

Step 5: Edgestitch around burp cloth

Starting at a corner, edgestitch around the burp cloth, making sure to backstitch as you start and stop.

Step 6: Fold diagonally and press

Fold the burp cloth in half diagonally and press along the fold. Open the fold.

Step 9: Create remaining burp cloths

Repeat steps 1–8 to create the additional burp cloths from the remaining FRONT and BACK pieces.

Step 7: Topstitch along fold line

Starting at one end of the fold, topstitch diagonally across the burp cloth on top of the fold line.

Step 8: Fold and topstitch

Repeat steps 6 and 7 to fold and topstitch diagonally between the remaining corners of the burp cloth.

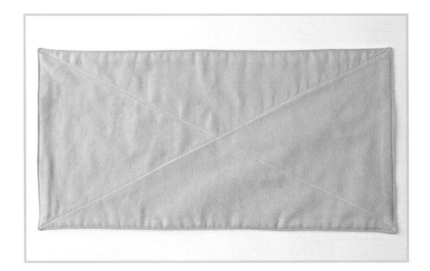

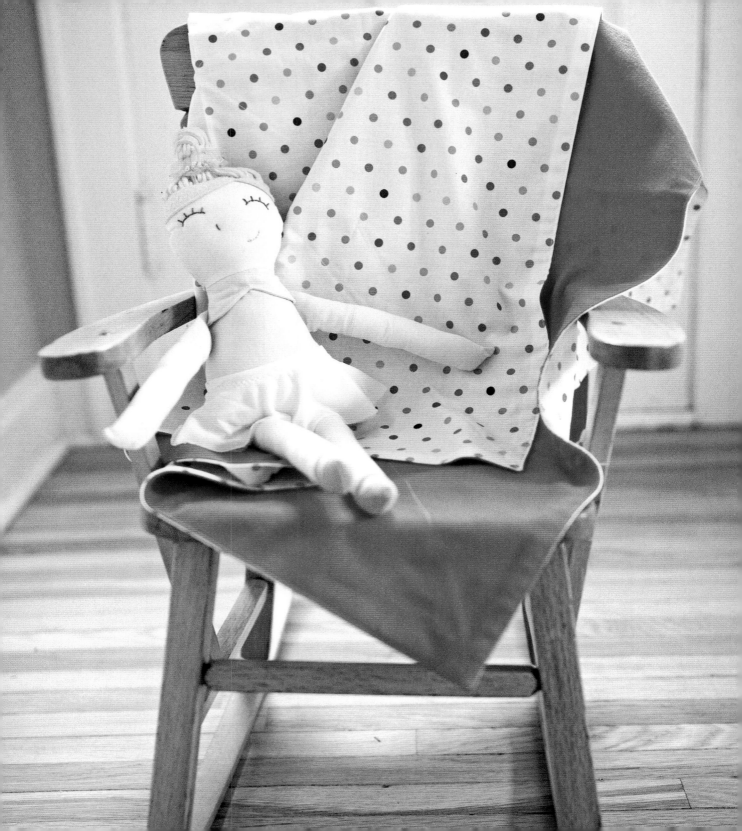

SWADDLING BLANKET

This baby blanket is perfect for bundling up your baby during any season. The flannel side is soft and cozy, while the cotton side will stay cool and fresh against your baby's skin. It's perfect for swaddling or draping over the car seat while your baby sleeps. You can also lay the blanket on the floor for a fast and easy play mat!

You will need:

- 1 yard quilting cotton for the FRONT
- 1 yard flannel for the BACK
- All-purpose thread

Yield: 1 swaddling blanket

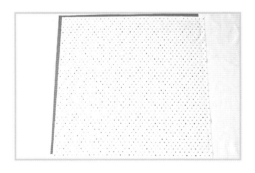

Prepare the following pieces:

FRONT—36˝ tall × 36˝ wide

BACK—36˝ tall × 36˝ wide

1

Step 1: Pin FRONT to BACK

With the FRONT and BACK right sides together, measure 12˝ from each corner along the bottom edge and pin. The space between these two pins will mark where the opening will be when you sew. Continue pinning around the blanket.

2

Step 2: Sew FRONT to BACK

Starting at one end of the opening, backstitch and sew around the blanket using a ½˝ seam allowance. Stop and backstitch at the other end of the opening.

3

Step 3: Clip corners

Snip off the corners of the blanket, making sure not to cut through the stitching.

4

Step 4: Turn blanket right side out and press

Turn the blanket right side out.

Use a chopstick to gently push the corners into place.

Press the blanket to keep the edges crisp. Keep the raw edges along the opening neatly tucked inside as you press.

Pin the opening shut.

5

Step 5: Edgestitch around blanket

Starting at a corner of the blanket, edgestitch around the blanket, making sure to backstitch as you start and stop.

6

Step 6: Fold the blanket diagonally and press

Fold the blanket in half diagonally and press along the fold. Open the fold.

Step 7: Topstitch along fold line

Starting at one end of the fold, topstitch diagonally across the blanket on top of the fold line.

Step 8: Fold blanket and topstitch along fold line

Repeat steps 6 and 7 to fold and topstitch diagonally between the remaining corners of the blanket.

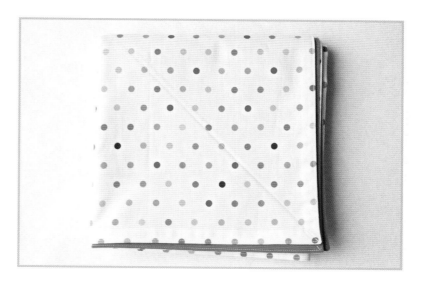

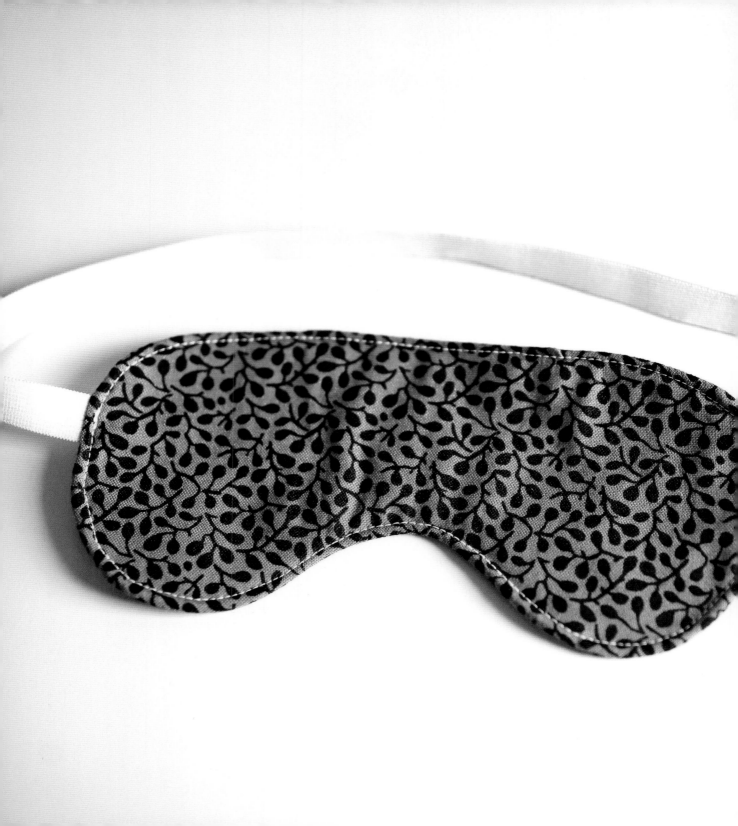

SLEEP MASK

What does every new mom and dad need more of? Sleep! Help them catch some much-needed Zzz's with this comfy slip-on sleep mask. The black lining hidden inside even helps block out the light so Mom and Dad can catch up on sleep any time of the day. Looking for a great baby shower idea? Pamper the new mom and her guests with an at-home spa, complete with handmade sleep masks and pedicures!

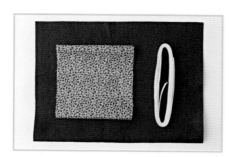

You will need:

- ⅛ yard quilting cotton for the FRONT and the BACK

- 1 sheet of black felt for the LINING

- 15″ of ½″-wide elastic for the ELASTIC BAND

- All-purpose thread

Tip: If you don't want to buy the full ⅛ yard of fabric, buy 1 fat quarter instead. Fat quarters of fabric typically measure about 18″ × 22″ and often come precut. If you can't find precut fat quarters at your fabric shop you can always ask if they'll cut one for you at the cutting counter.

Yield: 1 sleep mask

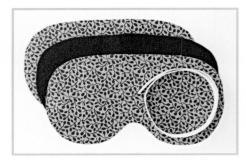

Prepare the following pieces:

Copy the SLEEP MASK pattern piece on page 181 according to the instructions for copying patterns on page 10. Use the copied SLEEP MASK pattern piece to cut the following pieces from fabric.

FRONT—cut from the SLEEP MASK pattern piece on fold

BACK—cut from the SLEEP MASK pattern piece on fold

LINING—cut from the SLEEP MASK pattern piece on fold

ELASTIC BAND—cut a 15″ piece of ½″-wide elastic

While the FRONT and BACK are still folded in half from cutting and the pattern is still in place, make a small snip at the opening mark on the top edge of the sleep mask. Also make two small snips to mark the ELASTIC BAND placement on the side of the sleep mask.

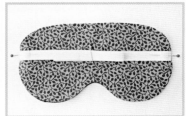

Step 1: Pin ELASTIC BAND to BACK and LINING

Place the BACK right side up on top of the LINING, matching the edges.

Pin each end of the ELASTIC BAND in between the two snips on each the side of the sleep mask. The ends of the ELASTIC BAND should be flush with the edges of the BACK when you pin. Be sure the ELASTIC BAND is not twisted.

Fold the middle section of the ELASTIC BAND on top of itself so it lies flat, and pin it in place in the center of the BACK with a safety pin so the elastic won't get caught as you sew.

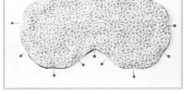

Step 2: Pin FRONT to BACK

Place the FRONT right side down on top of the ELASTIC BAND, BACK, and LINING, matching the edges.

Pin through all three layers of the sleep mask at each snip on the top edge. The space between these two pins will mark where the opening will be when you sew. Remove the pin from one end of the ELASTIC BAND and replace it with the pin going through all four layers. Repeat for the pin on the other end of the ELASTIC BAND.

Continue pinning around the sleep mask.

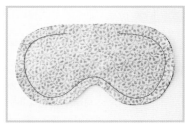

Step 3: Sew FRONT to ELASTIC BAND, BACK, and LINING

Starting at one end of the opening, backstitch and sew around the sleep mask using a ½″ seam allowance. Stop and backstitch at the other end of the opening. Go slowly and use the hand wheel as you sew around the curves.

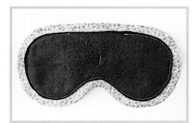

Step 4: Trim LINING

Turn the sleep mask over so the LINING is facing up. Trim the seam allowance of the LINING to ⅛″ along all sides.

5

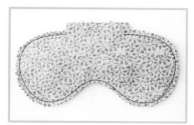

6

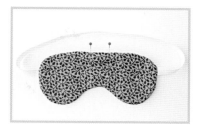

7

Step 5: Trim seam allowance on FRONT and BACK

Turn the sleep mask back over so the FRONT is facing up. Use pinking shears to trim the seam allowance of the FRONT and BACK to ⅛″ all the way around the sleep mask except across the opening. Do not trim the seam allowance across the opening.

Step 6: Turn sleep mask right side out and press

Turn the sleep mask right side out.

Use a chopstick to gently push the curves into place. Press the sleep mask to keep the edges crisp. Keep the raw edges along the opening neatly tucked inside as you press.

Pin the opening shut.

Step 7: Edgestitch around sleep mask

Edgestitch around the sleep mask, making sure to backstitch as you start and stop.

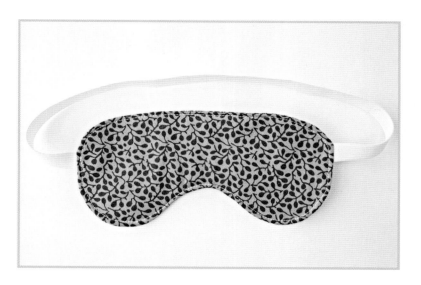

Finished!

DOOR BUMPER

This simple door bumper is perfect for keeping noisy door latches quiet so you can check on your sleeping baby without waking her up. Keep them on your doors as your baby grows to keep little fingers from getting smashed when a door closes. This door bumper is so fast and easy to make, you can make one for as many doors as you like! Or just make a few and move them from door to door as needed. The slip-on elastic loops won't damage the door or leave any markings behind.

You will need:

- ⅛ yard quilting cotton for the FRONT and the BACK

- 10″ of ½″-wide elastic for the LOOPS

- Stuffing

- All-purpose thread

Tip: If you don't want to buy the full ⅛ yard of fabric, buy 1 fat quarter instead. Fat quarters of fabric typically measure about 18″ × 22″ and often come precut. If you can't find precut fat quarters at your fabric shop you can always ask if they'll cut one for you at the cutting counter.

Yield: 1 door bumper

Prepare the following pieces:

FRONT—3 ½″ tall × 6″ wide

BACK—3½″ tall × 6″ wide

LOOPS—cut 2 pieces of ½″-wide elastic to 5″ long

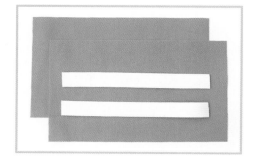

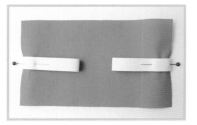

Step 1: Pin LOOPS to BACK

Fold one LOOP in half with the ends together.

With the right side of the BACK facing up, pin the ends of the LOOP to the BACK in the middle of the left edge (1½˝ from the top and bottom edges). Repeat with the remaining LOOP on the right edge.

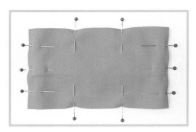

Step 2: Pin FRONT to BACK

Place the FRONT right side down on top of the BACK, with the edges aligned.

The LOOPS will be sandwiched in between the FRONT and the BACK. Remove the pin from each of the LOOPS one at a time, and replace it with the pin going through all three layers.

Measure 2˝ from each corner along the bottom edge and pin. The space between these two pins will mark where the opening will be when you sew. Continue pinning around the door bumper.

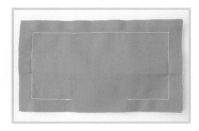

Step 3: Sew FRONT to BACK

Starting at one end of the opening, backstitch and sew around the door bumper using a ½˝ seam allowance. Stop and backstitch at the other end of the opening.

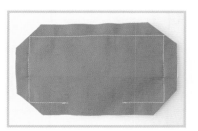

Step 4: Clip corners

Snip off the corners of the door bumper, making sure not to cut through the stitching.

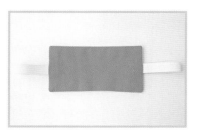

Step 5: Turn door bumper right side out and press

Turn the door bumper right side out.

Use a chopstick to gently push the corners into place.

Press the door bumper to keep the edges crisp. Keep the raw edges along the opening neatly tucked inside as you press.

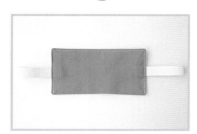

Step 6: Edgestitch along top and sides

Edgestitch along the left side, across the top, and along the right side of the door bumper, making sure to backstitch as you start and stop. Do not edgestitch across the bottom.

Step 7: Fill door bumper with stuffing

Fill the door bumper with stuffing until it is about 1˝ tall at the center.

Step 8: Pin opening shut

Pin the opening shut. See the instructions on page 9 for inserting pins into stuffed items. As you pin, be sure to keep the stuffing well away from the bottom edge.

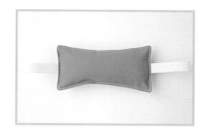

Step 9: Edgestitch across bottom

Edgestitch across the bottom edge, making sure to backstitch as you start and stop. Be sure to keep the stuffing away from the bottom edge as you sew.

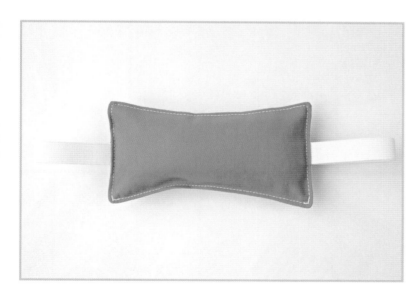

Finished!

Chapter Five
School Days

LUNCH SACK

If you love the simplicity of traditional paper lunch bags, but hate to throw them out, this simple lunch sack is the perfect compromise. It's sturdier and holds more than a paper sack and, of course, you can use it again and again. Fill it up with all your favorite lunchtime goodies, fold the top over, and add a clothespin or binder clip to keep it tidy until it's time to eat.

You will need:

- ⅓ yard quilting cotton for the OUTER
- ⅓ yard quilting cotton for the LINING
- All-purpose thread

Yield: 1 lunch sack

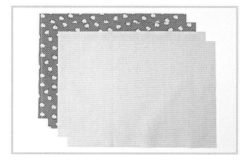

Prepare the following pieces:
OUTER FRONT and BACK—15″ tall × 11″ wide

LINING FRONT and BACK—15″ tall × 11″ wide

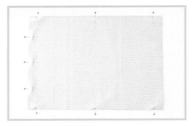

Step 1: Pin OUTER FRONT to OUTER BACK

Place the OUTER FRONT on top of the OUTER BACK with the right sides together. Pin along the top, bottom, and left side.

Step 2: Sew OUTER FRONT to BACK

Sew across the bottom, along the left side, and across the top of the OUTER FRONT and BACK using a ½˝ seam allowance, making sure to backstitch as you start and stop.

Step 3: Prepare boxed corner

Pull the OUTER FRONT and BACK apart at the center and reposition and flatten the bag so the side seams are lined up directly on top of each other. Find the actual tip of one corner (not the tip of the seam allowance) and align the tip of the corner with the point where two lines intersect on the cutting mat. Position your rotary cutting ruler diagonally on top of the corner with the ruler positioned 2˝ away from the corner tip on either side.

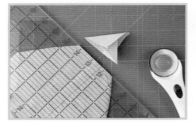

Step 4: Cut boxed corner

Cut the corner off by cutting along the edge of the ruler.

Step 5: Pin boxed corner

Pin across the cut edge.

Step 6: Sew across boxed corner

Sew across the corner ½˝ away from the cut edge, making sure to backstitch as you start and stop.

Step 7: Trim boxed corner

Trim the seam allowance along the cut edge to ⅛˝.

Step 8: Sew remaining corner

Repeat steps 3–7 for the remaining corner.

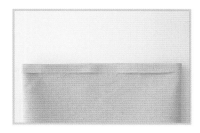

Step 9: Fold and press opening

Fold the open edge over ½˝ along the top of the OUTER and press.

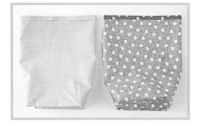

Step 10: Create LINING

Repeat steps 1–9 to create the LINING.

Step 11: Turn OUTER right side out and press

Turn the OUTER right side out and press.

Do not turn the LINING right side out.

Step 12: Pin LINING inside OUTER

Insert the LINING inside the OUTER. Match the side seams, bottom corners, and the fold along the opening, and pin the lining in place all the way around the opening.

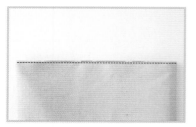

Step 13: Edgestitch around opening

Start at a side seam and edgestitch around the entire opening of the lunch sack, making sure to backstitch as you start and stop. The purpose of this edgestitching is to attach the LINING to the OUTER. Do not sew the opening shut.

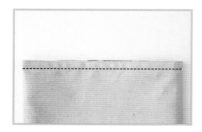

Step 14: Topstitch around opening

Topstitch around the entire opening of the lunch sack ½″ away from the edge of the fold, making sure to backstitch as you start and stop. This extra row of stitching will add to the strength of your lunch sack.

Finished!

LUNCH NAPKINS

Using fabric napkins at lunchtime not only cuts down on paper waste, it also encourages good manners. Make a stack of napkins with fun prints to send along in school lunches, or sew up a sophisticated set to bring in your lunches for work. They're so fun to use, you just might need a set to keep at home!

You will need:

- ⅓ yard quilting cotton
- All-purpose thread

TIP: If you don't want to buy the full ⅓ yard of fabric, buy 1 fat quarter instead. Fat quarters of fabric typically measure about 18″ × 22″ and often come precut. If you can't find precut fat quarters at your fabric shop you can always ask if they'll cut one for you at the cutting counter.

Yield: 1 napkin

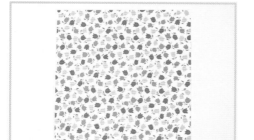

Prepare the following pieces:

NAPKIN—12″ tall x 12″ wide

1

Step 1: Fold top edge and press

With the wrong side of the fabric facing up, fold the top edge over ½˝ and press.

2

Step 2: Fold edge again, press, and pin

Fold the top edge over another ½˝ and press. Pin the fold in place.

3

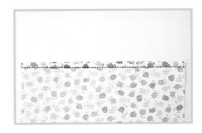

Step 3: Sew top edge

With the wrong side of the napkin facing up, edgestitch along the bottom of the fold, making sure to backstitch as you start and stop.

4

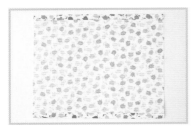

Step 4: Fold and sew bottom edge.

Repeat steps 1–3 for the bottom edge of the napkin.

5

Step 5: Fold and press side edge

Turn the NAPKIN so one of the side edges is now facing up. Fold this edge over ½˝ and press.

6

Step 6: Turn corners under

Unfold the fold you just pressed.

Fold the corner in so the tip of the corner touches the fold line you just made. Press the corner in place.

Repeat on the opposite corner.

Step 7: Refold and press

Refold along the original fold line, this time with the corners tucked neatly underneath.

Step 8: Fold side edge again and pin

Fold the side edge over another ½″ and press. Pin the fold in place.

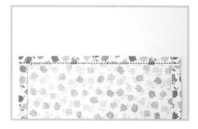

Step 9: Sew side edge

With the wrong side of the napkin facing up, edgestitch along the bottom of the fold, making sure to backstitch as you start and stop.

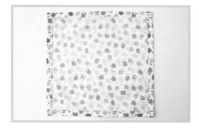

Step 10: Fold and sew opposite side edge

Repeat steps 5–9 for the opposite side edge.

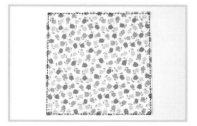

Step 11: Edgestitch around NAPKIN

Turn the NAPKIN over so the right side of the fabric is facing up. Starting at a corner, edgestitch around the entire napkin, making sure to backstitch as you start and stop.

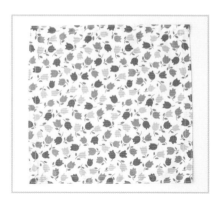

Finished!

PENCIL POUCH

Keep your child's backpack organized by corralling all of their favorite pencils in this simple pencil pouch. Make one for regular pencils and pens and another for colored pencils!

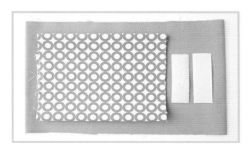

You will need:

- ⅛ yard quilting cotton for the OUTER
- ⅛ yard quilting cotton for the LINING
- 2 ½˝ of ¾˝-wide Velcro
- All-purpose thread

Tip: If you don't want to buy the full ⅛ yard of fabric for the OUTER or LINING, buy 1 fat quarter for each instead. Fat quarters of fabric typically measure about 18˝ × 22˝ and often come precut. If you can't find precut fat quarters at your fabric shop you can always ask if they'll cut one for you at the cutting counter.

Yield: 1 pencil pouch

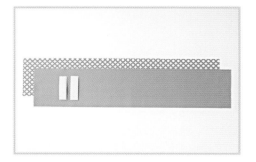

Prepare the following pieces:

OUTER—20˝ tall × 4˝ wide

LINING—20˝ tall × 4˝ wide

Velcro—cut a 2½˝ long piece

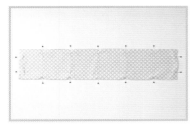

Step 1: Pin OUTER to LINING

With the OUTER and LINING right sides together, measure 1˝ from each corner along the right edge and pin. The space between these two pins will mark where the opening will be when you sew. Continue pinning around the pencil pouch.

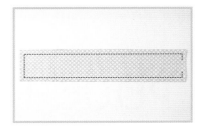

Step 2: Sew OUTER to LINING

Starting at one end of the opening, backstitch and sew around the pencil pouch using a ½˝ seam allowance. Stop and backstitch at the other end of the opening.

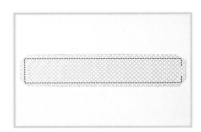

Step 3: Clip corners

Snip off the corners of the pencil pouch, making sure not to cut through the stitching.

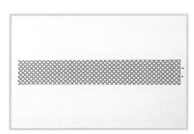

Step 4: Turn pencil pouch right side out and press

Turn the pencil pouch right side out.

Use a chopstick to gently push the corners into place.

Press the pencil pouch to keep the edges crisp. Keep the raw edges along the opening neatly tucked inside as you press.

Step 5: Pin opening shut

Pin the opening shut.

Step 6: Edgestitch across open edge

Edgestitch across the open edge, making sure to backstitch as you start and stop.

Step 7: Pin loop side of Velcro

Position the loop (soft) piece of Velcro 2˝ down from the sewn edge (centered on the pencil pouch), and pin it in place.

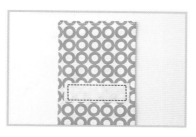

Step 8: Edgestitch around the Velcro

Edgestitch all the way around the Velcro twice, making sure to backstitch as you start and stop.

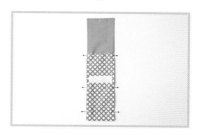

Step 9: Fold fabric to create a pouch

With the LINING facing up, fold the sewn edge of the pencil pouch up 7½˝ and pin in place, making sure to carefully match the side edges as you pin.

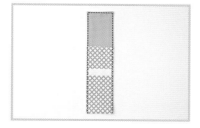

Step 10: Edgestitch around pencil pouch

Edgestitch all the way along the left side, across the top, and along the right side, making sure to backstitch as you start and stop. Do not sew across the bottom edge.

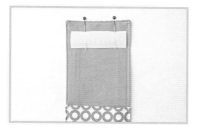

Step 11: Pin hook side of Velcro

With the LINING facing up, position the hook (scratchy) piece of Velcro ½˝ down from the top edge (centered on the pencil pouch), and pin it in place.

Step 12: Edgestitch around Velcro

Edgestitch all the way around the Velcro twice, making sure to backstitch as you start and stop.

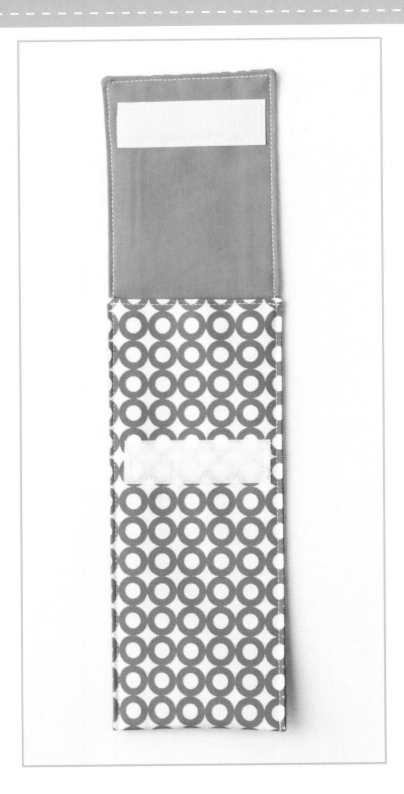

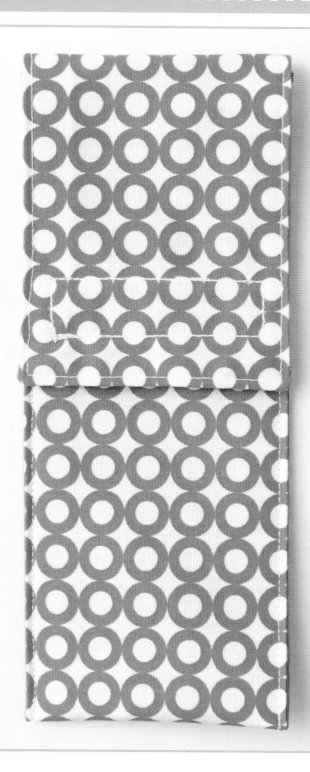

Finished!

Fill it up with all of your favorite pencils and fold the top flap down to keep them in place!

JOURNAL COVER

Transform a plain old composition notebook into a nice new journal with this quick and easy journal cover. Once the notebook is inside its cozy little cover, use the front and back flaps of the cover as pockets to store loose papers and other keepsakes. Perfect for use at school or at home!

You will need:

- ¼ yard quilting cotton for the OUTER
- ¼ yard quilting cotton for the LINING
- All-purpose thread

Yield: 1 journal cover

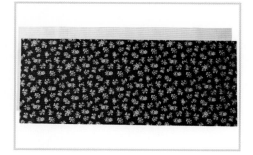

Prepare the following pieces:

OUTER—11 ¼˝ tall × 26 ½˝ wide

LINING—11 ¼˝ tall × 26 ½˝ wide

1

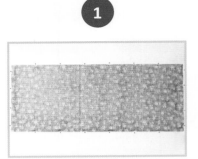

Step 1: Pin OUTER to LINING

With the OUTER and LINING right sides together, measure 3½″ from each corner along the right edge and pin. The space between these two pins will mark where the opening will be when you sew. Continue pinning around the journal cover.

2

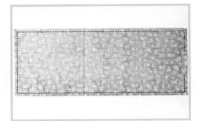

Step 2: Sew OUTER to LINING

Starting at one end of the opening, backstitch and sew around the journal cover using a ½″ seam allowance. Stop and backstitch at the other end of the opening.

3

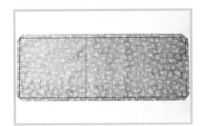

Step 3: Clip corners

Snip off the corners of the journal cover, making sure not to cut through the stitching.

4

Step 4: Turn journal cover right side out and press

Turn the journal cover right side out.

Use a chopstick to gently push the corners into place.

Press the journal cover to keep the edges crisp. Keep the raw edges along the opening neatly tucked inside as you press.

Pin the opening shut.

5

Step 5: Edgestitch along left and right sides

Edgestitch along the left side of the journal cover, making sure to backstitch as you start and stop. Do the same along the right edge. Do not edgestitch across the top or bottom edges.

6

Step 6: Fold sides in and pin

With the LINING facing up, fold the left side of the journal cover over 5 ½″ and pin it in place along the top and bottom edges. Do the same for the right side.

Step 7: Edgestitch across top and bottom edges

Edgestitch all the way across the top of the journal cover, making sure to backstitch as you start and stop. Do the same all the way across the bottom edge.

Step 8: Open journal cover

Open the journal cover so the LINING is facing up.

Step 9: Insert journal

Insert the front cover of a composition notebook into the left pocket on the journal cover. Carefully bend the composition notebook open and slip the back cover of the composition notebook into the right pocket of the journal cover.

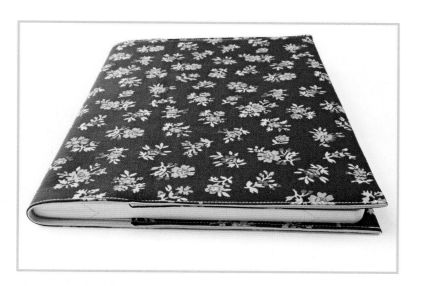

Finished!

POCKET HAND WARMERS

Little hands can get chilly walking to and from school or the bus stop in the cold winter months. Keep those chilly hands warm with these sweet little pocket hand warmers. Just pop them in the microwave for a minute or two and slip them into your child's pockets before heading out the door. When their hands get cold all they'll have to do is reach into their pockets to keep cozy and warm.

SCHOOL DAYS

You will need:

- ⅛ yard flannel
- ½ cup uncooked rice
- All-purpose thread

Yield: 2 hand warmers

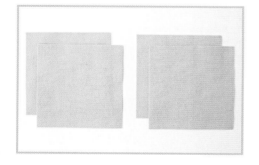

Prepare the following pieces:

FRONT—4″ tall × 4″ wide (cut 2 pieces)

BACK—4″ tall × 4″ wide (cut 2 pieces)

CHAPTER FIVE

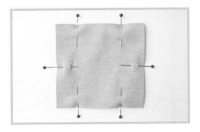

Step 1: Pin FRONT to BACK

With one of the FRONT pieces and one of the BACK pieces right sides together, measure 1″ from each corner along the bottom edge and pin. The space between these two pins will mark where the opening will be when you sew. Continue pinning around the hand warmer.

Step 2: Sew FRONT to BACK

Starting at one end of the opening, backstitch and sew around the hand warmer using a ½″ seam allowance. Stop and backstitch at the other end of the opening.

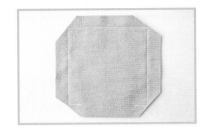

Step 3: Clip corners

Snip off the corners of the hand warmer, making sure not to cut through the stitching.

Step 4: Turn hand warmer right side out and press

Turn the hand warmer right side out.

Use a chopstick to gently push the corners into place.

Press the hand warmer to keep the edges crisp. Keep the raw edges along the opening neatly tucked inside as you press.

Step 5: Edgestitch along top and sides

Edgestitch along the left side, across the top, and along the right side of the hand warmer. Do not edgestitch across the bottom.

Step 6: Fill hand warmer with rice

Fill the hand warmer with ¼ cup uncooked rice.

Step 7: Pin opening shut

Pin the opening shut. See the instructions on page 9 for inserting pins into stuffed items. As you pin, be sure to keep the rice well away from the bottom edge.

Step 8: Edgestitch across bottom

Edgestitch across the bottom edge, making sure to backstitch as you start and stop. Be sure to keep the rice away from the bottom edge as you sew.

Step 9: Create second hand warmer

Repeat steps 1–8 to create the second hand warmer.

Finished!

To use: Warm up the hand warmers in the microwave for 1–2 minutes. Slip them into your pockets before heading out into the cold to keep your hands toasty warm!

Chapter Six

Toys

SOFT PLAY CAMERA

This soft play camera is quick and easy to make and oh-so-fun for your tiny photographer! Sew one up and your kids will be snapping away in no time!

You will need:

- ⅛ yard quilting cotton for the FRONT and the BACK

- Black felt for the DISPLAY SCREEN and the LENS

- White felt for the FLASH

- Assorted small felt pieces for the TRIGGER BUTTON, and the BUTTONS

- 10″ of ½″-wide twill tape for the WRIST STRAP

- Stuffing

- All-purpose thread

Tip: If you don't want to buy the full ⅛ yard of fabric, buy 1 fat quarter instead. Fat quarters of fabric typically measure about 18″ × 22″ and often come precut. If you can't find precut fat quarters at your fabric shop you can always ask if they'll cut one for you at the cutting counter.

Yield: 1 play camera

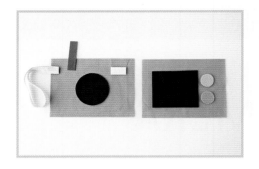

Prepare the following pieces:

Copy the CAMERA LENS and CAMERA BUTTON pattern pieces on page 181 according to the instructions for copying patterns on page 10. Use the copied pattern pieces to cut the CAMERA LENS and CAMERA BUTTONS from felt.

FRONT and BACK—4″ tall × 5½″ wide

DISPLAY SCREEN—2½″ tall × 3″ wide

LENS—cut 1 from the CAMERA LENS pattern piece

FLASH—½″ tall × 1″ wide

TRIGGER BUTTON—2″ tall × ½″ wide

BUTTONS—cut 2 from the CAMERA BUTTON pattern piece in different colors

WRIST STRAP—cut a 10″ long piece of ½″ wide twill tape

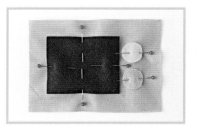

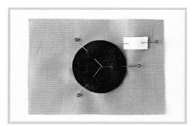

Step 1: Pin DISPLAY SCREEN and BUTTONS onto BACK

Place the DISPLAY SCREEN and the BUTTONS onto the BACK according to the placement guide on page 149, and pin them in place.

Step 2: Sew DISPLAY SCREEN and BUTTONS onto BACK

Starting at the bottom right corner, edgestitch all the way around the DISPLAY SCREEN, making sure to backstitch as you start and stop.

Edgestitch around each of the BUTTONS, starting at the bottom of each button and making sure to backstitch as you start and stop. When edgestitching around the BUTTONS, go slowly, and use the hand wheel.

Step 3: Pin LENS and FLASH onto FRONT

Place the LENS and the FLASH on the FRONT according to the placement guide on page 149, and pin them in place.

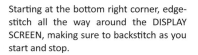

Step 4: Sew the LENS and FLASH onto the FRONT

Starting at the bottom, edgestitch all the way around the LENS, making sure to backstitch as you start and stop. When edgestitching around the LENS, go slowly and use the hand wheel.

Starting at the bottom right corner, edgestitch all the way around the FLASH, making sure to backstitch as you start and stop.

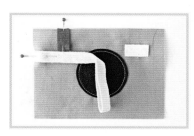

Step 5: Pin WRIST STRAP and TRIGGER BUTTON onto FRONT

Fold the TRIGGER BUTTON in half with the ½″ ends matched. Pin the ends of the TRIGGER BUTTON to the top edge of the FRONT according to the placement guide on page 149.

Fold the WRIST STRAP in half with the ½″ ends matched. Pin the ends of the WRIST STRAP in place along the left edge of the FRONT according to the placement guide. Fold the WRIST STRAP down over the LENS to keep the WRIST STRAP out of the way while sewing the camera together.

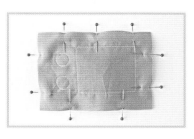

Step 6: Pin FRONT to BACK

Place the BACK right side down on top of the FRONT with the edges aligned.

Measure 1½″ from each corner along the bottom edge and pin. The space between these two pins will mark where the opening will be when you sew.

Continue pinning around the camera. When you come to the TRIGGER BUTTON, remove the pin already in place and replace the pin so it goes through the TRIGGER BUTTON, FRONT, and BACK. Do the same for the wrist strap.

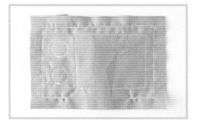

Step 7: Sew FRONT to BACK

Starting at one end of the opening, backstitch and sew around the camera using a ½″ seam allowance. Stop and backstitch at the other end of the opening.

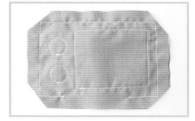

Step 8: Clip corners

Snip off the corners of the camera, making sure not to cut through the stitching.

Step 9: Turn camera right side out and press

Turn the camera right side out.

Use a chopstick to gently push the corners into place. Press the edges of the camera to keep the edges crisp. Do not press the felt. Keep the raw edges along the opening neatly tucked inside as you press.

Step 10: Edgestitch top and sides

Edgestitch along the left side, across the top, and along the right side of the camera, making sure to backstitch as you start and stop. Do not edgestitch across the bottom.

Step 11: Fill with stuffing

Fill the camera with stuffing until the camera is about 1˝ tall at the center.

Step 12: Pin opening shut

Push the stuffing away from the bottom edge and pin the opening shut. See the instructions on page 9 for inserting pins into stuffed items.

Step 13: Edgestitch across bottom edge

Edgestitch across the bottom edge, making sure to backstitch as you start and stop. Be sure to keep the stuffing away from the bottom edge as you sew.

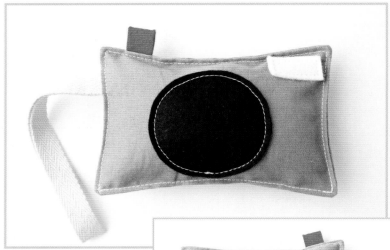

Finished!

BACK VIEW

PLAY CAMERA PLACEMENT GUIDE

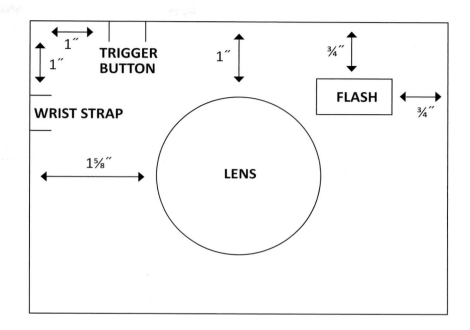

FRONT

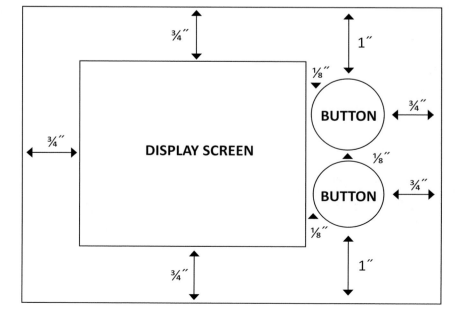

BACK

CHALK MAT & ERASER

With a full side for coloring and a back pocket to store the chalk and eraser, this fun little chalk mat is perfect for home use or travel. Use it for writing practice, drawing, or for playing games like tic-tac-toe. Pack it in your carry-on bag for trips or toss it in the church bag. It's a great quiet activity that's sure to keep those busy little hands happy.

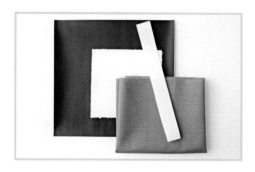

You will need:

- ¼ yard quilting cotton for the FRONT, BACK, and POCKET
- ¼ yard chalk cloth for the CHALK CLOTH
- ⅛ yard terrycloth for the ERASER FRONT and BACK
- 7˝ of ¾˝-wide Velcro
- All-purpose thread

Before you begin, read the information on sewing with chalk cloth in the fabric section on page 6.

Yield: 1 chalk mat and 1 eraser

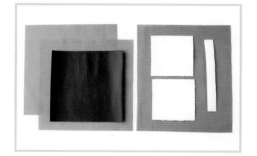

Prepare the following pieces:

CHALK MAT FRONT and BACK—9˝ tall × 9˝ wide

POCKET—10½˝ tall × 9˝ wide

CHALK CLOTH—7˝ tall × 7˝ wide

Velcro—cut a 7˝ long piece

ERASER FRONT and BACK—4˝ tall x 4˝ wide

Step 1: Fold POCKET

Fold the POCKET in half, wrong sides together and press the fold. The pocket should now measure 5¼˝ tall × 9˝ wide.

Step 2: Edgestitch along folded edge

Edgestitch along the folded edge of the POCKET, making sure to backstitch as you start and stop.

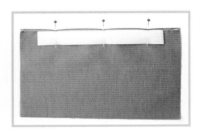

Step 3: Pin loop side of Velcro to POCKET

With the back side of the POCKET facing up, position the top edge of the loop (soft) piece of Velcro 5˝ above the bottom edge of the POCKET and 1˝ in from each of the side edges. Pin the loop side of the Velcro in place.

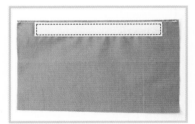

Step 4: Edgestitch around Velcro

Edgestitch all the way around the Velcro twice, making sure to backstitch as you start and stop.

Step 5: Pin hook side of Velcro to BACK

With the BACK right side up, position the top edge of the hook (scratchy) piece of Velcro 5˝ above the bottom edge of the BACK and 1˝ in from each side edge. Pin the hook side of the Velcro in place.

Step 6: Edgestitch around Velcro

Edgestitch all the way around the Velcro twice, making sure to backstitch as you start and stop.

Step 7: Attach POCKET to BACK

With the BACK facing right side up, place the POCKET (Velcro side down) on top of the BACK, making sure the bottom and side edges are aligned. The hook and loop pieces of the Velcro should align and stick together.

Step 8: Pin chalk cloth to FRONT

With the FRONT right side up, center the CHALK CLOTH on top of the FRONT, 1″ in from each side. Pin the CHALK CLOTH in place by inserting the pins through the CHALK CLOTH ⅛″ in from the edge of the CHALK CLOTH. Do not stick the pins back up through the CHALK CLOTH or you will have little holes left from the pins. Instead, stick the pins back up only through the FRONT, with the tip of each pin sandwiched in between the FRONT and the CHALK CLOTH. Pin this way all the way around the CHALK CLOTH.

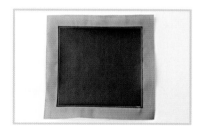

Step 9: Sew CHALK CLOTH to FRONT

Starting at the bottom right corner, edge-stitch around the CHALK CLOTH, making sure to backstitch as you start and stop.

Step 10: Pin FRONT to BACK

Make sure the POCKET is attached to the BACK as indicated in step 7. With the FRONT and BACK right sides together, measure 2″ from each corner along the top edge and pin. The space between these two pins will mark where the opening will be when you sew. Continue pinning around the chalk mat. As you pin, be careful not to pin through the CHALK CLOTH.

Step 11: Sew FRONT to BACK

Starting at one end of the opening, backstitch and sew around the chalk mat using a ½″ seam allowance. Stop and backstitch at the other end of the opening.

Step 12: Clip corners

Snip off the corners of the chalk mat, making sure not to cut through the stitching.

TOYS

SIMPLE SEWING

13

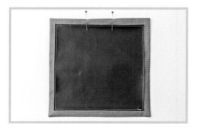

Step 13: Turn chalk mat right side out and press edges

Turn the chalk mat right side out. Be very careful with the CHALK CLOTH as you do this, making sure not to crease the CHALK CLOTH.

Use a chopstick to gently push the corners into place.

With the FRONT facing up, press only the edges of the chalk mat to keep the edges crisp. Do not press the CHALK CLOTH. Keep the raw edges along the opening neatly tucked inside as you press. Turn the chalk mat over and iron the BACK quickly, making sure the iron doesn't rest on the middle of the chalk mat for longer than a couple of seconds. This will allow you to iron the BACK of the chalk mat without ruining your CHALK CLOTH. Pin the opening shut.

14

Step 14: Edgestitch around mat

Starting at the bottom right corner, edgestitch around the chalk mat, making sure to backstitch as you start and stop. The chalk mat is now finished.

15

Step 15: Pin ERASER FRONT to BACK

With the ERASER FRONT and BACK right sides together, measure 1″ from each corner along the bottom edge and pin. The space between these two pins will mark where the opening will be when you sew. Continue pinning around the eraser.

16

Step 16: Sew FRONT to BACK

Starting at one end of the opening, backstitch and sew around the eraser using a ½″ seam allowance. Stop and backstitch at the other end of the opening.

17

Step 17: Clip corners

Snip off the corners of the eraser, making sure not to cut through the stitching.

18

19

Step 18: Turn eraser right side out and press

Turn the eraser right side out.

Use a chopstick to gently push the corners into place. Press the eraser to keep the edges crisp. Keep the raw edges along the opening neatly tucked inside as you press.

Pin the opening shut.

Step 19: Edgestitch around eraser

Starting at a corner, edgestitch around the eraser, making sure to backstitch as you start and stop.

Finished!

BACK VIEW

MEMORY GAME

Collect all of your favorite fabric scraps and use them to create your own handmade version of this classic memory game. Great for children of all ages!

You will need:

- ¼ yard quilting cotton for the BACK pieces

- 10 large scraps or 10 pieces of ⅛ yard each of quilting cotton for the FRONT pieces

- All-purpose thread

Tip: Choose a dark color to use for the back of the memory game tiles so all the fun prints you choose for the matches won't show through the back.

Yield: 20 memory game tiles (10 matched pairs)

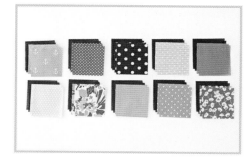

Prepare the following pieces:

BACK—3˝ tall × 3˝ wide (cut 20 pieces)

FRONT—3˝ tall × 3˝ wide (from 10 different fabrics, cut 2 pieces each)

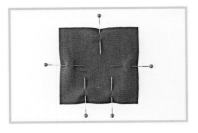

Step 1: Pin FRONT to BACK

With one of the FRONT pieces and one of the BACK pieces right sides together, measure 1˝ from each corner along the bottom edge and pin. The space between these two pins will mark where the opening will be when you sew. Continue pinning around the memory game tile.

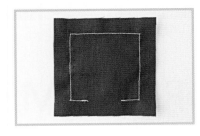

Step 2: Sew FRONT to BACK

Starting at one end of the opening, backstitch and sew around the tile using a ½˝ seam allowance. Stop and backstitch at the other end of the opening.

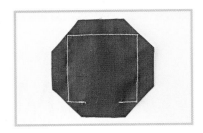

Step 3: Clip corners

Snip off the corners of the tile, making sure not to cut through the stitching.

Step 4: Turn tile right side out and press

Turn the tile right side out.

Use a chopstick to gently push the corners into place. Press the tile to keep the edges crisp. Keep the raw edges along the opening neatly tucked inside as you press. Pin the opening shut.

Step 5: Edgestitch around tile

Starting at a corner, edgestitch around the tile, making sure to backstitch as you start and stop.

Step 6: Create remaining tiles

Repeat steps 1–5 to create the remaining 19 tiles.

Finished!

How to play:

Start by mixing up the memory game tiles with the back of each tile facing up.

Lay the tiles out in rows with the backs facing up.

Take turns turning over two tiles at a time. If the two tiles don't match, turn them back over and return them to their original places so you can remember where they are. When you find a match, place the matched tiles in a separate pile.

Continue taking turns turning over the tiles until all the matches have been found.

BEAN BAGS

Bean bags are perfect for children of all ages and for so many different activities! Throw them, catch them, aim them at a target—this simple bean bag is so quick and easy to sew, you'll want to make a whole basketful!

You will need:

- ⅛ yard quilting cotton for the FRONT and the BACK
- ⅓ cup dry beans
- All-purpose thread

Tip: If you don't want to buy the full ⅛ yard of fabric, buy 1 fat quarter instead. Fat quarters of fabric typically measure about 18″ × 22″ and often come precut. If you can't find precut fat quarters at your fabric shop you can always ask if they'll cut one for you at the cutting counter.

Yield: 1 bean bag

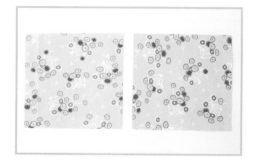

Prepare the following pieces:

FRONT—5″ tall × 5″ wide

BACK—5″ tall × 5″ wide

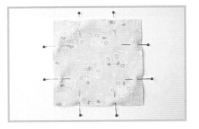

Step 1: Pin FRONT to BACK

With the FRONT and BACK right sides together, measure 1 ½″ from each corner along the bottom edge and pin. The space between these two pins will mark where the opening will be when you sew. Continue pinning around the bean bag.

Step 2: Sew FRONT to BACK

Starting at one end of the opening, backstitch and sew around the bean bag using a ½″ seam allowance. Stop and backstitch at the other end of the opening.

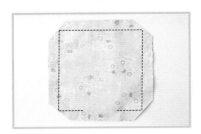

Step 3: Clip corners

Snip off the corners of the bean bag, making sure not to cut through the stitching.

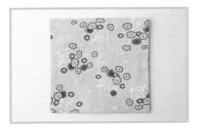

Step 4: Turn bean bag right side out and press

Turn the bean bag right side out.

Use a chopstick to gently push the corners into place. Press the bean bag to keep the edges crisp. Keep the raw edges along the opening neatly tucked inside as you press.

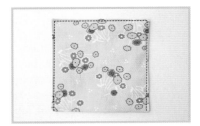

Step 5: Edgestitch along top and sides

Edgestitch along the left side, across the top, and along the right side of the bean bag, making sure to backstitch as you start and stop. Do not edgestitch across the bottom.

Step 6: Fill bean bag with beans

Fill the bean bag with ⅓ cup dry beans.

Step 7: Pin opening shut

Pin the opening shut. See the instructions on page 9 for inserting pins into stuffed items. As you pin, be sure to keep the beans well away from the bottom edge.

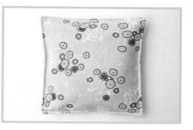

Step 8: Edgestitch across bottom

Edgestitch across the bottom edge, making sure to backstitch as you start and stop. Be sure to keep the beans away from the bottom edge as you sew.

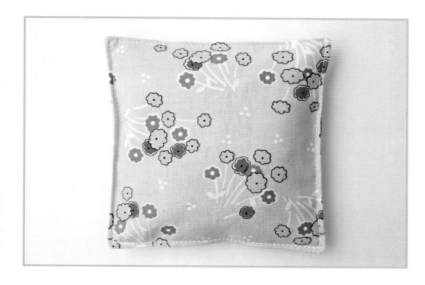

Finished!

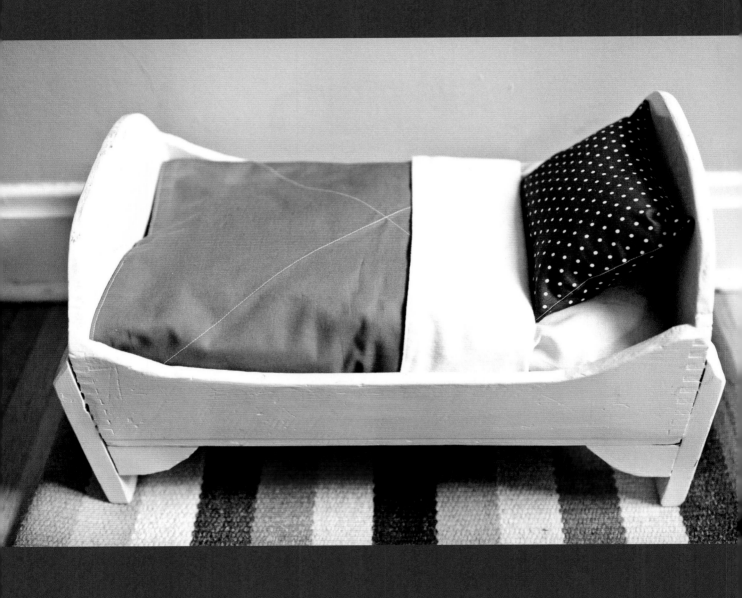

BABY DOLL PILLOW & BLANKET

This sturdy little pillow and blanket set are perfect for keeping your baby doll cozy in her bed. The pillow is perfectly squishy and soft for her to rest her little head on, and the blanket is reversible!

You will need:

- ¼ yard quilting cotton for the PILLOW

- ½ yard flannel or quilting cotton for the BLANKET FRONT

- ½ yard flannel or quilting cotton for the BLANKET BACK

- Stuffing

- All-purpose thread

TIP: If you don't want to buy the full ½ yard of fabric for each side of the blanket, buy 1 fat quarter for each instead. You can also make the pillow from 1 fat quarter. Fat quarters of fabric typically measure about 18″ × 22″ and often come precut. If you can't find precut fat quarters at your fabric shop you can always ask if they'll cut one for you at the cutting counter.

Yield: 1 baby doll pillow and blanket

Prepare the following pieces:

PILLOW FRONT and BACK—7″ tall × 9″ wide

BLANKET FRONT and BACK—18″ tall × 18″ wide

1

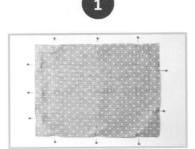

Step 1: Pin PILLOW FRONT to BACK

With the PILLOW FRONT and BACK right sides together, measure 2″ from each corner along the right edge and pin. The space between these two pins will mark where the opening will be when you sew. Continue pinning around the pillow.

2

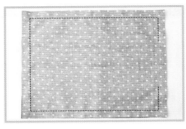

Step 2: Sew PILLOW FRONT to BACK

Starting at one end of the opening, backstitch and sew around the pillow using a ½″ seam allowance. Stop and backstitch at the other end of the opening.

3

Step 3: Clip corners

Snip off the corners of the pillow, making sure not to cut through the stitching.

4

Step 4: Turn pillow right side out and press

Turn the pillow right side out.

Use a chopstick to gently push the corners into place. Press the pillow to keep the edges crisp. Keep the raw edges along the opening neatly tucked inside as you press.

5

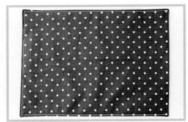

Step 5: Edgestitch along bottom, top, and left side

Starting at the bottom right corner, edgestitch across the bottom, along the left side, and across the top of the pillow. Do not edgestitch across along the right side.

6

Step 6: Fill pillow with stuffing

Fill the pillow with stuffing until the pillow is about 2″ tall at the center.

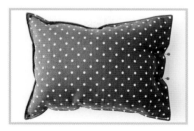

Step 7: Pin opening shut

Push the stuffing away from the right edge and pin the opening shut. See the instructions on page 9 for inserting pins into stuffed items.

Step 8: Edgestitch along right edge

Edgestitch along the right edge, making sure to backstitch as you start and stop. Be sure to keep the stuffing away from the right edge as you sew. The pillow is now finished.

Step 9: Pin BLANKET FRONT to BACK

With the BLANKET FRONT and BACK right sides together, measure 6˝ from each corner along the bottom edge and pin. The space between these two pins will mark where the opening will be when you sew. Continue pinning around the blanket.

Step 10: Sew FRONT to BACK

Starting at one end of the opening, backstitch and sew around the blanket using a ½˝ seam allowance. Stop and backstitch at the other end of the opening.

Step 11: Clip corners

Snip off the corners of the blanket, making sure not to cut through the stitching.

Step 12: Turn blanket right side out and press

Turn the blanket right side out.

Use a chopstick to gently push the corners into place.

Press the blanket to keep the edges crisp. Keep the raw edges along the opening neatly tucked inside as you press.

Pin the opening shut.

13

Step 13: Edgestitch around blanket

Starting at the bottom right corner, edgestitch around the blanket, making sure to backstitch as you start and stop.

14

Step 14: Fold blanket diagonally and press

Fold the blanket in half diagonally and press along the fold. Open the fold.

15

Step 15: Topstitch along fold line

Starting at one end of the fold, topstitch diagonally across the blanket on top of the fold line.

16

Step 16: Fold the blanket and topstitch along the fold

Repeat steps 14 and 15 to fold and topstitch diagonally between the remaining corners of the blanket.

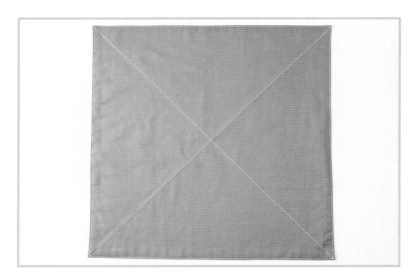

Finished!

Patterns

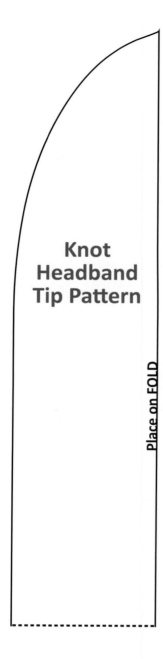

Knot Headband Tip Pattern

Place on FOLD

The bottom edge is a dashed line, because it is NOT used for cutting.

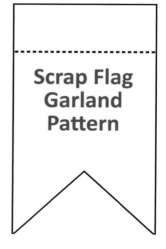

Scrap Flag Garland Pattern

The dotted line indicates where the piece should be folded after it's cut.

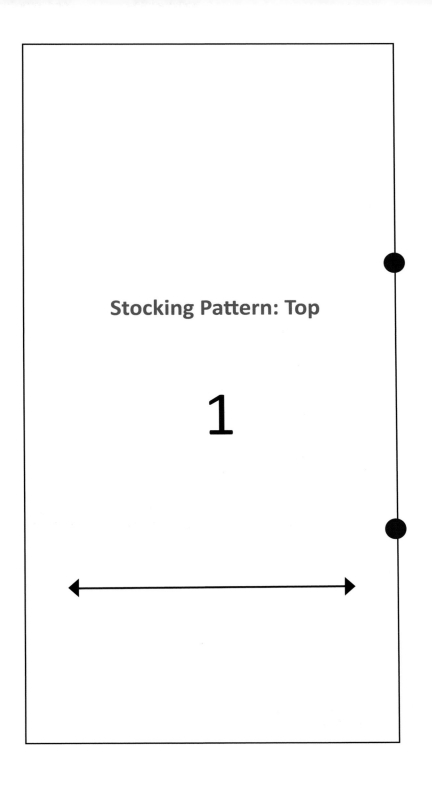

Stocking Pattern: Top

1

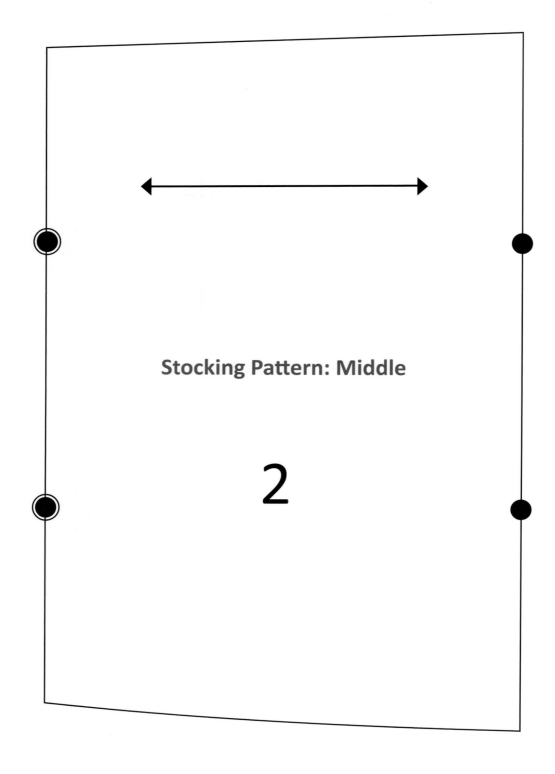

Stocking Pattern: Middle

2

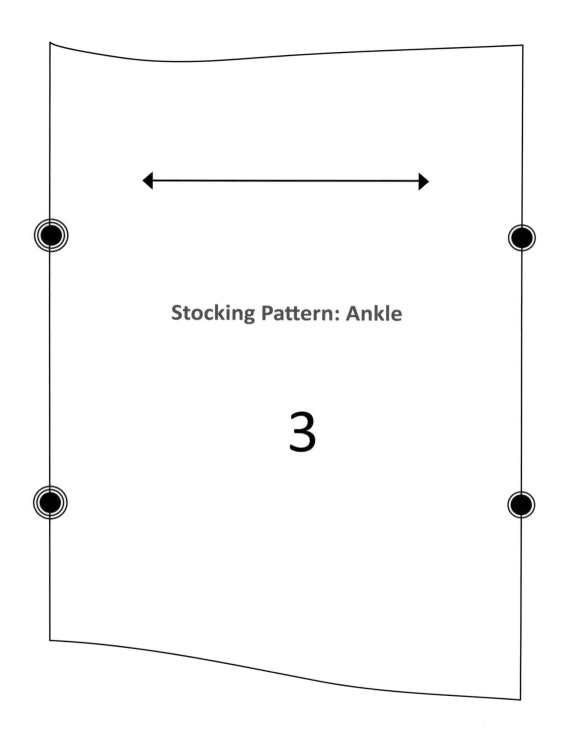

Stocking Pattern: Ankle

3

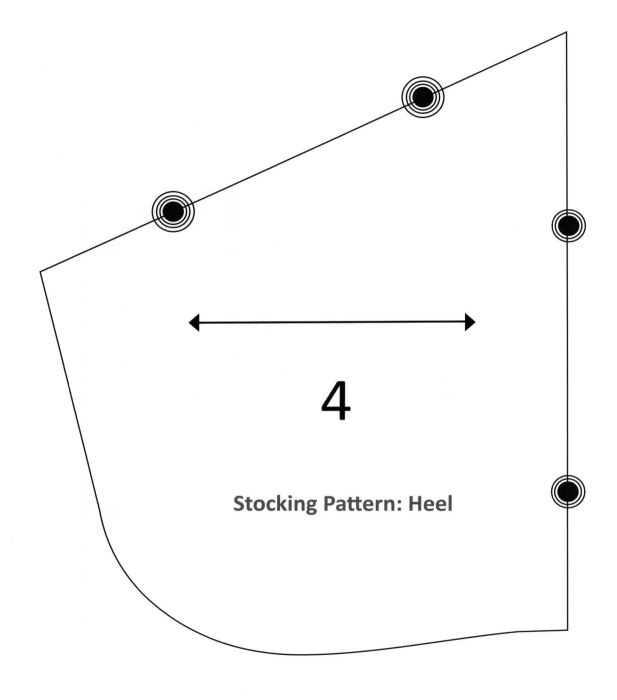

4

Stocking Pattern: Heel

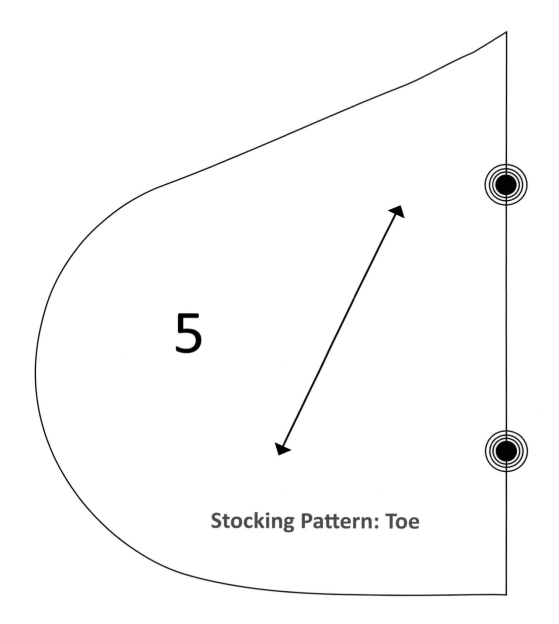

5

Stocking Pattern: Toe

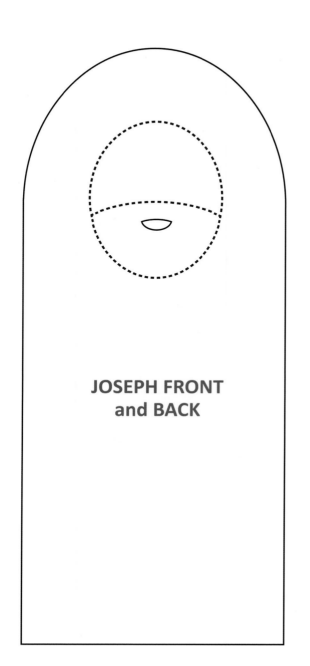

**JOSEPH FRONT
and BACK**

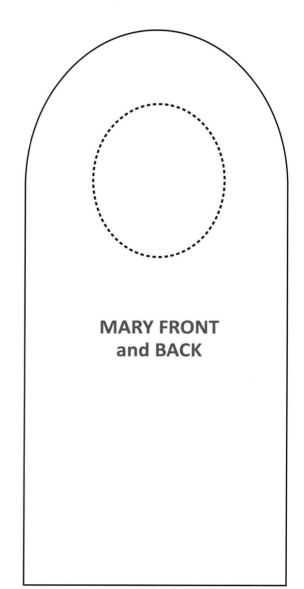

**MARY FRONT
and BACK**

Felt Nativity Puppets Pattern

The dotted lines are a guide to show where the face
should be placed when sewing the pieces together.

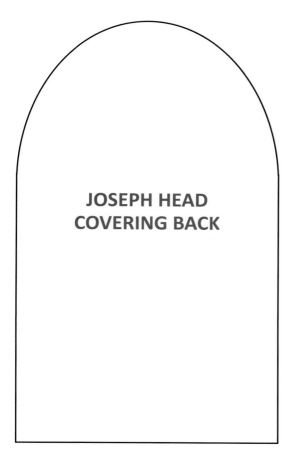

JOSEPH HEAD COVERING BACK

JOSEPH AND MARY HEAD COVERING FRONT

JOSEPH AND MARY FACE

MARY HEAD COVERING BACK

JOSEPH BEARD

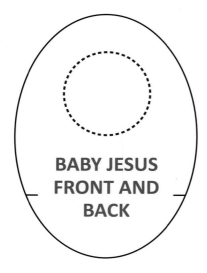

BABY JESUS FRONT AND BACK

The dotted line is a guide to show where the face should be placed when sewing the pieces together.

BABY JESUS BLANKET

BABY JESUS FACE

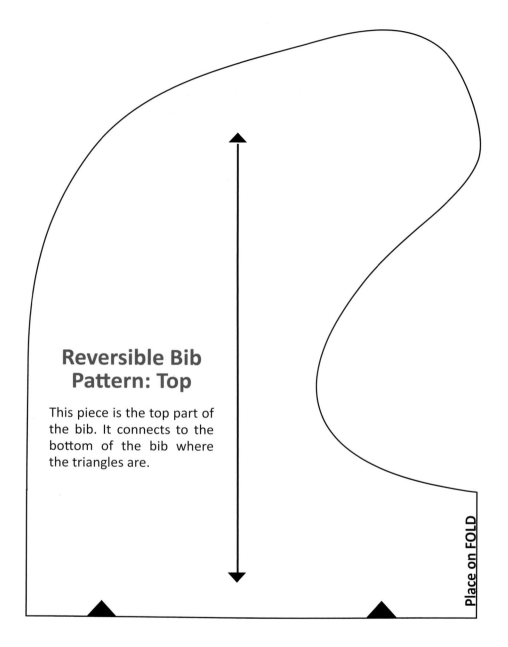

Reversible Bib
Pattern: Top

This piece is the top part of the bib. It connects to the bottom of the bib where the triangles are.

Place on FOLD

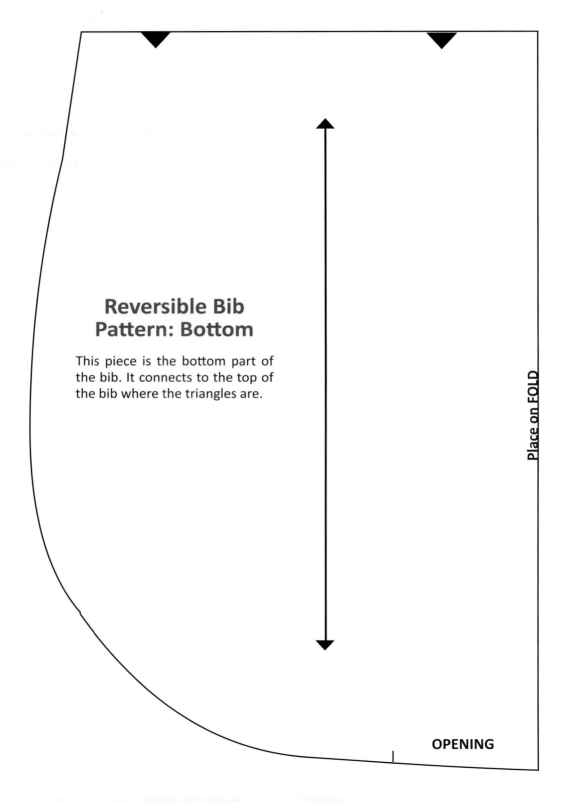

Reversible Bib
Pattern: Bottom

This piece is the bottom part of the bib. It connects to the top of the bib where the triangles are.

Place on FOLD

OPENING

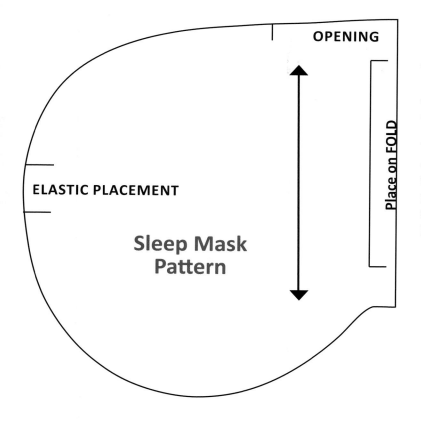

OPENING

Place on FOLD

ELASTIC PLACEMENT

Sleep Mask Pattern

The small vertical line at the top is to mark where the opening will be when you sew. Make a small snip at this line while your pieces are still folded in half.

The small horizontal lines on the left side of the pattern piece are to mark where the elastic will be pinned and sewn in place on the sleep mask. Make a small snip at each of these lines while your pieces are still folded in half.

Play Camera Pattern

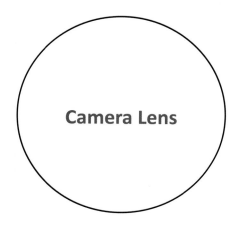

Camera Lens

Camera Button

About the Author

KATIE LEWIS graduated from Brigham Young University with a degree in home and family living. She first learned how to sew as a child in her mother's makeshift sewing room and this early love of creating has continued throughout her life. She writes regularly on her blog, *The Red Kitchen* (www.the-red-kitchen.com), about crafts, sewing, and life as a mom. She currently lives in Columbus, Ohio, where she teaches local sewing classes and bakes a lot of chocolate chip cookies.